THE NEW MIRACLE DYNAMICS
Amazing Power for Daily Living

Other Books by Theodor Laurence
Satan, Sorcery and Sex
Helping Yourself with Spells, Prayers, Curses and
  Chants
The Miracle Power of Believing
Helping Yourself with Psychosymbology

THE NEW MIRACLE DYNAMICS
Amazing Power for Daily Living

THEODOR LAURENCE

Parker Publishing Company, Inc.   West Nyack, N.Y.

This book is a reference work based on research by the
author. The opinions expressed herein are not necessarily
those of or endorsed by the Publisher.

Library of Congress Cataloging in Publication Data

Laurence, Theodor.
   The new miracle dynamics.

   1. Success. I. Title.
BJ1611.2.L42   131   81-9488
ISBN 0-13-615088-8   AACR2

For Beverly, who demonstrates continually with unbounded gratitude.

Where there is no vision, the people perish.
Proverbs 29:18

What New Miracle Dynamics Will Do for You And for Everyone You Touch

You are in the right place at the right time.

That is why you are reading these words.

If you can believe the above statement, you *are* the right person in the right place at the right time. And miracles are in store for you because of this Truth.

Who Should Read this Book

If

- You believe the only way to make money is by the sweat of your brow or through worry and vain hope . . .
- You believe ill health is natural and normal and is caused by outer conditions . . .
- You believe that sorrow and misery are simply one's lot in life these days . . .
- You believe successful people have "better breaks" than you do . . .
- You believe luck is capricious and uncontrollable . . .
- You believe love and joy and friendship and peace merely "happen" to some and not to others . . .

Then this book will show you how to dispel this kind of thinking that deprives you of all the good things in life.

And if

- You sense, however dimly, that there is a "secret" to attracting fabulous sums of money to yourself . . .
- You believe health—perfect and eternal health—is the birthright of every person . . .
- You sense, through intuition, that there is a key to the thorough banishment of sorrow and misery . . .
- You believe you can be as successful and as rich as others . . .
- You can mentally create an image of luck as an onflowing, ongoing influx of goodness . . .
- You strongly desire love and joy and friendship and peace . . .

Then this book is for you!

A New, Miracle-Working Power Is at Your Fingertips Right Now

If you have a need, a problem, an unfilled desire . . . if you are experiencing a setback, an obstacle, an obstruction to your success and happiness . . . then take a good hard look at it and kiss it goodbye! It will no longer exist by the time you have completed *The New Miracle Dynamics*.

The New Miracle Dynamics gives you the answers you've been looking for—amazing power for daily living, power that can transform your life into what you'd like it to be. This book will show you how to easily and quickly transform even the worst conditions into happy circumstances. You will learn to master any situation that causes you suffering. You will learn to change any pattern of living that deprives you of the best. In the following electric pages, you will find and *use* the secret of shape-shifting, life-transforming power—a power that means the same thing as Cosmic Mind or God—*New Miracle Dynamics*.

Revealed at Last! The Mystic Secret of Psycho-Image Materialization

But I'm not asking you simply to take my word that new Miracle Dynamics holds the key to all good fortune. Here's how you can put the prime method technique of Psycho-Image to work—to work wonders in your daily life:

Psycho-Image: You have just received a check for $10,000. You walk to the bank, you deposit the check in your account, and you receive a brand new checkbook that reflects your deposit. You return home, you sit down comfortably, and you start making out checks. You pay all those worrisome bills and mail your checks, freeing yourself of troublesome burdens. Then you go out and visit a big department store. You look about you like a king surveying his kingdom— anything you want is at your beck and call. You move around the counters and purchase all the things you ever wanted and needed. You purchase for yourself, for your loved ones, for your friends. Maybe you even buy something for a complete stranger, just to be charitable. And smiling faces—yours included—appear everywhere in your new life! *This is New Miracle Dynamics in action.*

Psycho-Image: Your employer comes up to you and says: "I have a confession to make. I've misjudged you and I have been abusing your energies and talents. Starting today you have a raise, and I am promoting you. You are much too valuable to me to be wasted on this work-horse labor." Suddenly you are recognized, valued, appreciated. You go to work from this day forward as if floating two feet off the ground, your heart full, your energy flowing freely and powerfully, and for the first time in years you feel wanted, joyful, positive, and effective. *This is New Miracle Dynamics in action.*

Psycho-Image: You awaken one morning to find that you are at your healthiest. A glance in the mirror shows you a whole, healthy, energetic, vigorous person with bright, shining eyes, glowing complexion, and radiant features. There is new spring to your step, new enthusiasm in your outlook, new charisma to your personality. Wherever you walk, people turn to look at you, to admire you, to show their warmth toward you. New acquaintances and new friends seem to appear miraculously, surrounding you, filling your days and nights with love and friendship and companionship. You are amazingly healthy, strong, and popular. You can feel health-giving and health-promoting energy coursing through your veins, your limbs, your heart, your every cell. You are whole! *This is New Miracle Dynamics in action.*

Psycho-Image: A strange new power is yours. You walk among those who, until now, have denigrated you, reviled you, picked on you. With your new power you "zap" them. *Presto!* Instantly, you are loved, esteemed, admired! With your new power you change negativity into positivity, destructiveness into constructiveness, dearth into plenty, loneliness into popularity, evil into good. Wherever you go, people, circumstances, conditions, and patterns are altered for the better. Evil influences, dark thoughts, dreadful enemies—all these disappear as if by magic, and you are released from their former hold on you; you are liberated, set free! *This is New Miracle Dynamics in action.*

The Secret Power of Psycho-Image Materialization Is Now Yours!

What is this "Psycho-Imaging" that creates miracles? It is *Psycho-Image Materialization.* "Psycho-Image" means Mental Picture, and "Materialization" is the outpicturing of your wishes, dreams, and desires. PSYCHO-IMAGE MATERIALIZATION is the magical process by which you will bring into your actual experience whatever you are thinking about!

Psycho-Image Materialization is a new and exciting psychospiritual technique of Mind Power through which you, and you alone, *create* what you want out of life and *receive* it!

A "Psycho-Image" is a creatively constructed scene enacted upon the stage of your own mind. By an act of will and/or intense desire, you set this stage; you place the actors and actresses; you write the script. In short YOU ARE THE

DIRECTOR! The secret lies in the word "Materialization." You will make your thoughts *materialize*. According to Webster, *materialize* means:

1. To give material form or characteristics to; represent in material form.
2. To make (a spirit, etc.) appear in bodily form.
3. To become fact; develop into something real or tangible; be realized.

In other words, you will make your fancies facts, your dreams realities, your wishes experiences, your desires tangible truths. This book will show you exactly how to use this amazing, new, miracle-working power in your own life. You will be filled with joy!

The Wisdom of the Ages Comes to Twentieth-Century You!

Psycho-Image Materialization is new, yet the principle behind it is one of the oldest and most secret powers discovered by man. Jesus Christ used it, Buddha used it, all great Teachers used it. It is this cosmic power principle that inspired such great men and women as the following: Einstein ("Imagination is more important than knowledge"); Mary Baker Eddy ("God is Mind, and God is infinite; hence all is Mind"); Milton ("The mind is its own place, and in itself/Can make a heaven of hell, a hell of heaven"); Seneca ("As the soil, however rich it may be, cannot be productive without culture, so the mind without cultivation can never produce good fruit"); Thoreau ("Man is the artificer of his own happiness"); and countless other men and women of wisdom and insight. Today, thousands of people just like you are reaping full reward from this miracle secret, as proven by the real-life testimonies in this book, and it is this same power principle that you will use through *Psycho-Image Materialization*. Christ said that the things He did you would do—*and greater!* Now is the time to do so! Take advantage of age-old wisdom and modern scientific knowledge by absorbing the contents of this book and putting the power of PSYCHO-IMAGE MATERI-ALIZATION to work in your own life.

Modern scientific inquiry has confirmed ancient mystical truth: *the power of your mind can work miracles!* Scientific exploration of the human mind has unleashed a seemingly new power potential: the human ability to change and control physical matter through the powers of mind and thought. This is the basic principle that underlies and empowers *psycho-image materialization*, and this book will show you how to activate it in your own private life, for your own private use. This book is not merely a teacher; it is your friend, and so is its author, both of whom are dedicated to your health, happiness, and increased success. Together—you, I, and this book—will work now to create joyful and happy miracles in *your* life!

Everything you need is already provided for you—all you have to do is reap a harvest of riches!

This book provides you with all you will ever need to activate and employ your new power of PSYCHO-IMAGE MATERIALIZATION. The only thing you bring to it is your heartfelt *desire* for more out of this life. Therefore, for your immediate benefit you will find in each chapter the following:

1. Step-by-step instructions—easy to read and easy to use—showing you how to get the most out of *New Miracle Dynamics*.

2. *Psycho-Image Materialization Affirmations:* power words that will cut through any problems and influences that block your way to efficient and joyful experience and that will prepare the fertile soil of your subconscious mind for greater, more fulfilling activity in your life.

3. *New Miracle Mind Activators:* potent "Psycho-Images" that will raise the vibratory rate of your own thoughts to that pitch that induces all good to come into your experience.

4. *Case Histories* of people just like yourself that illus-

trate exactly how PSYCHO-IMAGE MATERI-
ALIZATION will work in your life to bring you
riches, love, fun, excitement, health, prosperity—
anything you want!

The Best Part of All

I've saved the best news for last! It answers the question: "What do I have to do to transform my thoughts into
concrete things, my wishes into reality, my dreams into actual experience?" Quite a question—and the answer will
amaze you, please you, and enrich you! The answer is: You do
nothing at all—*except desire*! The *Psycho-Image Materializer*
will do the rest!

Think about this! The universe's secret, hidden, helping
Power will provide you with whatever you want—
instantaneously—and all you have to do is THINK!

The *Psycho-Image Materializer* (often called God, Force,
Infinite Intelligence, and so on) is a universal Power ready
and willing to do your bidding. As with the Father in relation
to Jesus Christ, this universal Power wants you to have "every good thing." You deserve the best in life; you deserve
plenty, abundance, enrichment, prosperity, and success. This
great Power—the *Psycho-Image Materializer*— will respond
to your every need, here and now, with no delay, depending
upon your ability to trust IT, believe IT, and open to IT.

All you have to do is absorb the secrets of *Psycho-Image
Materialization* that are carefully outlined in this book and
mentally picture and ardently desire whatever you want or
need; and *automatically, synchronistically, spontaneously,*
the *Psycho-Image Materializer* (the greatest Power this universe has ever known) will do the rest—the miracle-working
part! All you have to do is sit back and let riches and enjoyment flow freely into your new life.

Psycho-Imaging is the technique that will make the
Psycho-Image Materializer your devoted sponsor and friend,
ever ready to fulfill your wishes, dreams, and desires. This
book will show you how to easily and quickly befriend this
mighty, wonder-working force. You will then draw Its power

into your life, thereby receiving all that you rightly deserve, enriching yourself and succeeding where others fail and achieve little. With the Divine aid of Psycho-Image Materialization, you will reap a harvest of benefits that will delight you and amaze onlookers.

New Miracle Dynamics has brought joy and happiness into countless lives—now you can benefit, too!

This book contains scores of amazing case histories of people, just like you, who have used Psycho-Image Materialization to realize their dreams. Here is just a sampling:

- A Louisville, Kentucky man Psycho-Imaged his way out of abject poverty into gratifying riches. (Page 57).
- A sixty-year-old woman found impossible happiness through her use of the secrets revealed in Chapter Five.
- An Ohio man developed a "psychic radar" through Psycho-Image Materialization exercises that made him a successful and wealthy poker winner.
- A door-to-door salesman was led to a cache of riches by a ferocious dog, and the man discovered $150,000 worth of jewels!
- An Ohio cabdriver progressed from a penniless pauper to a man worth over $500,000.00 by employing the technique outlined in Chapter Eleven.
- A man won the heart of the beautiful girl he desired by using the four-step program outlined in Chapter Seven.
- An Arizona woman used Psycho-Image Materialization and mentalized herself into fabulous wealth.
- John D. had his sight restored; Sandra R. escaped breast surgery; Ken F. overcame sinus attacks—all through the Psycho-Image Materialization key to miraculous healing!
- A California man wanted to commit suicide, yet by using Psycho-Image Materialization programs he unearthed a container which concealed $50,000.00 and found happiness and joy!

Psycho-Image Materialization is an easy-to-use, but powerful method for realizing your hopes and dreams. The easy-to-follow instructions in this book will bring you a happy, rich and joyous life—*automatically*. Share with the thousands who are now using this new miracle-method to enrich and enhance their daily living.

Theodor Laurence

Contents

What New Miracle Dynamics Will Do for You and for Everyone You Touch 5

1. Activate New Miracle Dynamics Power for a Great New Life 23

Psycho-Image Materialization Affirmation #1   26

The Greatest Secret You Will Ever Learn About Attracting Miraculous Riches and Success to Yourself!   27

How to Make Abundance of Every Kind Start Flowing into Your Life Right Now   28

How Psycho-Image Materialization Enriches Your Life   29

How Two Ordinary People Changed Their Dull Existence Into Life More Abundant   30

What You Should Know About Your Image-Power   32

How a High School Drop-Out Became a Highly Paid Executive in a Huge Corporation   33

The Rock-in-the-Pool Image   34

The Secret of Transforming Negativity Into Positivity   35

Janet P. and the Crushing-Eye Psycho-Image   36

New Miracle Dynamics Mind Activator #1   37

If You Know What You Want, Nothing Is Stopping You from Obtaining It   38

New Miracle Dynamics Works to the Degree That You Disregard Appearances   39

Valuable Tips You Will Want to Remember   40

2. Obtain and Pyramid Mountains of Money Through Psycho-Image Materialization 43

What You Should Know About Money—Why You Don't Have It and How to Get All You Need   45

Psycho-Image Materialization Affirmation #2   46

How Bill M. Turned His Abject Poverty into Glorious Riches   47

New Miracle Dynamics Mind Activator #2   48
How He Did It   49
Our Needs and Circumstances Are Different But You Can Use
    the Same Technique that Bill M. Used   50
What Bill M. Has, You Can Have—and More!   52
The Secret of Psycho-Image Materialization Is Yours to Use
    and Enjoy   53
How Psycho-Image Materialization Transforms Lack into
    Plenty, Poverty into Riches, Dearth into Wealth   54
Joan L. Psycho-Imaged Herself Getting a Raise and Received a
    Miracle   54
How Carter P. Turned an Idle Wish into Exciting Reality   56
How Psycho-Image Materialization Lifted a Man out of Poverty
    and Lack   57
Money Is the Physical Manifestation of Spiritual Wealth   58
Know What You Want and Go After It   59
Others Are Getting What They Want: So Can You!   60
The New Miracle Dynamics Secret that Insures Your Receipt of
    Greater Riches   61

3. **How to Use the Psycho-Image Materialization Key to
   Miraculous Healing** 63

If You Do Not Know the Source of Health, You Can Lose It; if
    You Know the Source of Health, You Can Never Lose
    It!   65
The Psycho-Image Secret to Health, Vigor, and Vitality   66
Psycho-Image Materialization Affirmation #3   67
You Are Now Ready to Be Infused with Vitalizing
    Health-Energy   68
New Miracle Dynamics Mind Activator #3   69
How to Use Psycho-Image Materialization the Way Sandra L.
    Did to Heal Herself   70
Psycho-Image Materialization Brings Instant Health and
    Healing to You and Your Loved Ones   73
The Mystic Secret of Healing Now Revealed to You   75
How to Use Psycho-Image Materialization Across Great
    Distances for the Healing of Others   76
How Evelyn T. Used the "Healing Oil" Psycho-Image to Cure
    Her Chronic Arthritis   77
Your Miracle Method for Curing Arthritis   78
How a Woman Lost 88 Pounds Through the Secret of
    Psycho-Image Materialization   80

The New Miracle Dynamics Program for Losing Weight
Fast 80
How Supernatural Healing Aids Modern Medicine and
You 80
Your New Miracle Dynamics Key to Super Health 81
Put Yourself in this List of Miraculously Healed People 82
Supernatural Healing Is Really Natural—if It Isn't Happening
in Your Life, Something's Wrong 83

**4. Magnetize Unexpected Windfalls, Surprising Good Fortune,
and Phenomenal Luck** 85

Psycho-Image Materialization Affirmation #4 88
Invisible, Beneficent Forces Are Now Activating in Your
Life 90
New Miracle Dynamics Mind Activator #4 90
Use These Ten-Steps for Accruing Fast Riches 91
New Miracle Dynamics Makes Ancient Truths Work for You in
Modern Ways 94
The Mystic Secret of Psycho-Imaging Is Yours to Use and
Enjoy 99

**5. Attract, Command, and Enjoy Love, Respect, Honor, and
Fame the New Miracle Dynamics Way** 101

Psycho-Image Materialization Affirmation #5 103
Why the Secrets of Mysticism Confound the World 104
New Miracle Dynamics Mind Activator #5 105
How Cora, L. Found Supreme Happiness 106
How Psycho-Image Materialization Made Roger D. an
Irresistible Lady's Man 108
How New Miracle Dynamics Works Depends Upon Your
Desires 110

**6. The Amazing Power That Overcomes Enemies, Combats
Evil Thoughts, and Dispels Negative Influences** 113

Psychic Attack Calls for Emergency Defense 115
How Beatrice R. Was Being Slowly Vampirized by the Woman
Next Door 116
She Cried: "It Was Like Being Sucked Dry of My Blood!" 117
Why a Happy Groom Turned Into a Terrifying Monster 117
The Mystic Secret of New Miracle Dynamics Saves You From
Danger and Prevents Psychic Attack for All Time 118

Psycho-Image Materialization Affirmation #6   118
Raise Your Vibrations to the Plane of Light-Beings and Then
    Activate Supernatural Power to Help You   120
New Miracle Dynamics Mind Activator #6   120
They All Agree: "I Think I Would Have Died Without
    Psycho-Image Materialization"   122
How New Miracle Dynamics Gives You Fourth-Dimensional
    Aid and Protection Against Evil   123
Psycho-Image Materialization Protects You From the Greatest
    Terror of All   124

**7. Million-Dollar Personality and Irresistible Charm Through
    Psycho-Image Materialization** **127**

Psycho-Image Materializatoin Affirmation #7   130
Attraction Is Mental but Its Benefits Are Material   131
New Miracle Dynamics Mind Activator #7   132
Your Psycho-Image Materialization Exercise Works Miracles
    and Produces Spectacular Results   134
How Psycho-Image Materialization Made Jane R.'s Life a
    Cinderella Story   134
How Barry L. Became a Popular, Happy Lady's Man!   137
How Cindy F. Won the Man She Wanted Most   138
She Was Unmarried Because She Thought She Was Drab   139
How New Miracle Dynamics Increases Your Popularity   139

**8. Let Psycho-Image Materialization Magnify Your Personal
    Success Rate** **141**

The Secret to Magical Power Is No Secret to You!   143
How Don L. Used Psycho-Image Materialization to Rise Above
    Financial Crunch that Others Still Suffer   144
What Don Did, Anyone Can Do—Especially You   146
Psycho-Image Materialization Affirmation #8   147
Affirm, Open, and Get Ready to Receive More Than You Asked
    For!   148
A Few Simple Rules For Getting the Most Out of Your
    Psycho-Image Materialization Affirmation   148
New Miracle Dynamics Mind Activator #8   149
Her House Caught Fire, Her Car Blew Up, and She Wanted to
    Die   150
She Psycho-Imaged Her Success, and It Came to Her Within
    Four Hours!   152

9. **The Secret Force That Puts You in Command at All Times**..155

How To Become Super Confident—and Stay That Way   158
Psycho-Image Materialization Affirmation #9   158
How a Salesman Used Psycho-Image Materialization to
    Overcome His Self-Defeating Inferiority   159
New Miracle Dynamics Mind Activator #9   160
Jill S. Was a Loser Until She Practiced Psycho-Image
    Materialization   162
Psycho-Image Materialization Demonstrates That What
    Imprisons You Will Set You Free—If You let It!   164

10. **How to Control Thoughts and Feelings with New Miracle Dynamics** 165

Why the Image-Forming Part of Your Mind Will Work Like
    Magic for You   167
How Psycho-Image Materialization Gives You the Edge in All
    Human Affairs   168
How a Successful and Wealthy Poker Player Developed His
    "Psychic Radar"   169
Psycho-Image Materialization Affirmation #10   170
Change the Thoughts and Feelings of Others, and You Can't
    Lose   171
New Miracle Dynamics Mind Activator #10   172
How Timothy C. Was Subconsciously Helped to Attract the
    Sum of $40,000   176
You, Too, Can Manifest Your Desires Quickly and Easily   178

11. **The Secret of Forever Banishing Fears, Doubts, Setbacks, and Obstacles**......................................181

The Psycho-Image Materialization Secret to Inner and Outer
    Balance   183
Make a List of the People, Places, and Things Blocking You
    from Perfect Happiness   184
Pause Each Day to Show Gratitude Prior to Receipt   185
How a 16-Year-Old Girl Saved Her Brother's Life in a
    Miraculous Manner   186
How Richard M. Progressed from a Penniless Cab driver to a
    Man Worth Over $500,000   187
The Technique that Makes You a Conqueror and a Winner   189

Psycho-Image Materialization Affirmation #11   190
You Have Just Done Yourself the Biggest Favor in Your
    Life   191
New Miracle Dynamics Mind Activator #11   191
You Become a Partner in the Creation of Your New Life   195

12. Psycho-Image Materialization for Fun and Profit.........**197**

Psycho-Image Materialization Affirmation #12   200
Through the Magic of Psycho-Image Materialization, You
    Attract Fun and Pleasure on Command   200
Remember that Your Psycho-Images Are Requests and that
    Universal Mind Never Says No   202
How to Have a Great Deal of Fun and Pleasure While Your Life
    Is Improving Magically   202
New Miracle Dynamics Mind Activator #12   203
How a Woman's Psycho-Image Helped Her to Read the Mind of
    the Man She Desired   205
How Lisa D. Escaped a Life of Drudgery and Loneliness and
    Emerged Bright, Happy and Vivacious   207
Use Your New Psycho-Imagery Power to Brighten Your
    Life   208
Let New Miracle Dynamics Work for You and Enjoy a Totally
    New and Exciting Life   210

**13. Obtain Everything You Want, Need and Desire Through
    New Miracle Dynamics!** **213**

How to Take Full Advantage of the Secret of Psycho-Image
    Materialization for Your Own Benefit and Good   215
Amazing New Miracle Dynamics Works Wonders
    Instantaneously   216
Psycho-Image Materialization Affirmation #13   217
How to Encourage the Powerful Creative Force of the Universe
    to Produce Your Good   218
New Miracle Dynamics Mind Activator #13   219
Terry M. Wanted a Beautiful Girl and Employed
    Psycho-Imagery to Get What He Wanted   221
How Audrey B. Used Psycho-Image Materialization to Gain
    Fabulous Wealth   222
Apply New Miracle Dynamics, and You Will Have Your Heart's
    Desire   223

A Final Word About New Miracle Dynamics **225**

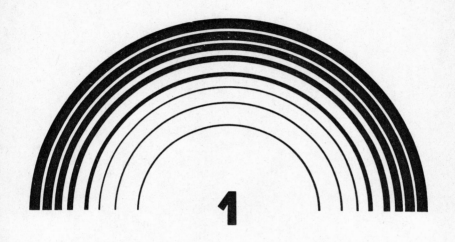

1

Activate New Miracle Dynamics Power for a Great New Life

As with everything else in this life, it is wise to begin at the beginning if we expect to do something correctly. So let's do that. Let's get into the proper state of mind, the state of consciousness that makes you a living magnet for all the good things you desire.

First of all, *know* that there *is* such a state of consciousness. It is the rockbed of New Miracle Dynamics. It is easy to attain. Simply follow these easy steps:

1. Get alone with yourself in a comfortable place. Close your eyes for a few moments, take a few deep breaths, close out of your mind all confusion, disturbance, and thoughts of inharmony. You are now indwelling peace and serenity and lake-clear consciousness.

2. Take just a few minutes to acknowledge something you may have forgotten or may never have known: There is a single Source of all you want out of life. It doesn't matter what you name this Source, but *know* It is higher than human. Some call It God, others Mind, still others Infinite Intelligence. The important thing is to recognize a Divine Agency above and beyond our finite minds. God likes acknowledgment; Mind responds to your recognition; Infinite Intelligence appreciates your notice. In religious terms, "your Father smiles upon you as you smile upon Him."

   In your comfortable and peaceful place, alone with all-embracing, all-encompassing Divine Presence, say the following affirmation vocally or mentally.

3. With your body comfortable in a position of calm repose, with your mind attuned to Infinite Mind, you are ready to receive according to your belief. If you believe small, you will receive small things; if you believe BIG, you will receive BIG things!

Psycho-Image Materialization Affirmation #1

There is a Divine Source of all that is. This Source is like a fluid that is in, through, and around everything. It is in, through, and around me right now. I am immersed in It, permeated by It, suffused with It. Even as I sit here, It is prepared to fill my every need, no matter what it is I ask for. I gladly recognize this Source of All, and in gratitude do I open myself to Its influx. I do so right now!

There is but One Source of all the good in the world. I am one with this Source. The power of this Agency is my own power, and I use it now to fulfill myself.

With gratitude do I accept all the wonderful things about to fill my life. I remain open and receptive, quiet and confident, and all I need is now materializing in my experience, drawing closer to me by the moment. I wait in humble expectation, thankful now for that which I do not yet see but know *is manifesting for me.*

My every wish and desire are being met at this very moment. I can feel it happening, and this excites me, thrills me, makes me happy. I let it be so. And so it is!

Your third step is *Psycho-Image Materialization* itself, the use of mental power to manifest in your life all you will ever need, want, desire, or wish for.

How do you do it? Well, let's take a look at what you *don't* do. You do not struggle, work, slave, or force. You do not fall on your knees and pray agonizing prayers to a far-off God-in-the-sky.

You are God ("I and my Father are One"), and the "sky" is your own heights of consciousness. What you do is "let go and let God," that is, you don't force gifts upon yourself, but sit quietly in a state of *receptive* consciousness and *permit* all the gifts to flow to you! They *will* flow to you if you *let* them. And *Psycho-Image Materialization* will help that flow to begin, increase, and overwhelm you with joy and happiness, riches, and success.

The Greatest Secret You Will Ever Learn About Attracting Miraculous Riches and Success to Yourself!

There is a *secret* to *Psycho-Image Materialization*. There is a *key* to attracting all you want, anytime you want it. This secret key is *gratitude prior to receipt*!

Gratitude is not sentimental thankfulness; it is a power principle! The best example of how this principle works is given in the life and actions of the Master Teacher, Jesus Christ. No one will deny that perhaps the most amazing miracle Jesus performed was the raising of Lazarus from the dead. You probably know the story well.

> *Then they took away the stone from the place where the dead was laid. And Jesus lifted up his eyes, and said, Father, I thank thee that thou hast heard me.*
> *And I knew that thou hearest me always . . .*
> *And when he thus had spoken, he cried with a loud voice, Lazarus, come forth.*
> *And he that was dead came forth.*
>
> John 11:41-44

Note well that Jesus did not thank the Father *after* Lazarus came forth, but *before* that miraculous event!

Whatever you Psycho-Image, *know* before you see your desire manifested that it will, indeed, manifest—without doubting! Be thankful *before* you see the fruit of your mental power. *Know* that Creative Mind, Infinite Intelligence, the Father, "hears you always"! *Gratitude prior to receipt* is the magical key to successful and miraculous use of *Psycho-Image Materialization*.

How to Make Abundance of Every Kind Start Flowing into Your Life Right Now

Let's start with you *just as you are*. If you are instructed to change first before you can use your new power, the power is worthless. No, a real and effective power must be at your disposal *here and now*. And so it is!

Pause and ask yourself an important question: Where am I right now? What kind of circumstances do I find myself in? In what spiritual condition am I?

Are you in need of money? Health? Love? Friendship? Luck? Personal power?

Let's begin with your need, your desire, your dream. You will soon discover that you already possess the key to their fulfillment. We all have it! It is simply that our minds are so preoccupied with the deficit that we fail to see the asset. Put another way, our spirit is so smothered by daily worries and troubles that it seems as if there is no way out of difficulty. But there is!

There is an illustrative story of a young East Indian who deeply desired to possess magic. In his pursuit of this great power he roamed the country, going from guru to guru, looking for the holy man who could imbue him with the power. One day, hungry and tired, almost hopeless of locating the right holy man, he was directed to seek out the Wise One on the hill. The "hill" happened to be about three miles straight up! The young man toiled and labored to conquer this mountain. He struggled ever upward, day and night, through brambles and thorns, eating berries and roots because he had neither food nor money. At long last he reached the place, his destination, and he stood laboring for breath, his dusty face turned toward a hovel in the trees.

He approached the hut, bent down, and entered the dark interior. When his eyes adjusted to the semi-darkness, what should he see but an old and decrepit man upon a pallet, almost dead! The ancient one lifted a feeble, bony hand and beckoned to the lad to draw closer. "At last," he said in a weak voice. "At last you have come. I have waited for years for this day."

The young man thought he was babbling in his illness. All he could say was: "I am amazed to see you like this. You do not appear as I pictured you."

"How did you picture me, young man?" asked the old man.

"Why . . . vigorous! Strong! Alive! Full of power and energy! I saw you youthful and exuberant and full of wisdom and teaching me magic!"

Suddenly the old man's face brightened with a strange, white light. His old eyes flamed with youth. His creaking limbs began to move easily. He leapt to his feet, laughing. He did a little jig in the dust and exclaimed: "Wonderful! Come! Let us eat and drink and praise God!"

The young man was consternated and stood gaping at the rejuvenated old man who now seemed younger and more spirited than himself. "I don't understand," he marveled, "I thought you were dying!"

"I was!" the guru laughed. "I might have, had it not been for you. I've been waiting for the Magic One to appear. And here you are!"

"I?" choked the young man.

"Of course, *you.* As you pictured me, so I am! That is magic. Did you not know that you possess the power?"

Did you know that you possess the power?

This question is now addressed to you, the reader! No, he did not know he possessed the magic power, nor do we if, like him, our troubles and worries obfuscate and over shadow it!

The same power the young man possessed, *you* possess: *Psycho-Image Materialization.* The mystic secrets to this wonder-working power are now yours in this book.

How Psycho-Image Materialization Enriches Your Life

What you Psycho-Image in your mind brings instant results in your outer conditions. Like a supernatural force in your subconscious, it reaches out an invisible arm to change circumstances, even when we are not aware of it. It works in such a way that no one would ever know the power was coming from you, and yet you emerge the victor, the conqueror, the blessed!

The subconscious mind makes real what you image!

Both ancient mystics and modern psychologists have mapped the trajectory of thought. In simple terms, what enters your subconscious mind as thought, comes back out as shape-shifting power. The moment your subconscious acts on your thought, will or desire, unseen powers come into play.

Your subconscious, however, unlike your conscious reasoning mind, accepts all Psycho-Images equally—and produces them! This is why *Psycho-Image Materialization* teaches you to use only positive, success-producing Psycho-Images.[1]

How Two Ordinary People Used Psycho-Image Materialization to Change Their Dull Existence Into Life More Abundant

Anna L. and Ralph S., both of Canton, Ohio, are typical examples of the thousands of men and women benefiting materially from Psycho-Images and supernatural help.

Anna at one time used every ounce of her energy just to get through a day of housework. Housecleaning had become a drudgery, and this drudgery was undermining her health and happiness. She changed all that miraculously with the secret power of Psycho-Image Materialization.

Ralph was in a similar situation, using himself up on a job that was overtaxing his energy and personality. He was being sapped of vitality and creativity. His job became the only thing in his life! Psycho-Image Materialization saved him from years of constant boredom and gifted him with a rich and successful life.

How did they do it?

First of all, they each got alone with themselves and prepared the receptivity of their subconscious with *Psycho-Image Materialization Affirmation #1.*

---

[1]See Theodor Laurence, *Helping Yourself With Psychosymbology* (West Nyack, New York: Parker Publishing Company, 1978).

Secondly, they *pictured it*! Anna pictured (Psycho-Imaged) herself "breezing" through housework. This dynamic Imagery worked immediately, the very next day, in fact. But the subconscious has more in store for you than finished housework!

Once Anna found drudgery a "breeze." the latent powers of her subconscious came to the fore. She suddenly "felt" that she should be enjoying much more of life. It was subconscious powers telling her this, already guiding her toward richer, fuller living.

The miracle occurred during Anna's Bingo evenings. Suddenly, inexplicably, Anna began to win, win, WIN! Other ladies who had been losing steadly along with Anna for many weeks couldn't believe this sudden change in fortune. They implored Anna to tell her secret. She shared it with some of them.

She told them about *Psycho-Image Materialization* and then revealed that right after reciting the *Affirmation*, she employs this chant:

> *Bingo circle, Bingo wheel,*
> *Let me money feel, feel, feel;*
> *Turn for me, stop for me*
> *Let me rich and wealthy be!*

Anna first turned a ten-dollar bill into $100. The following weekend she won $500! She started salting all this money away. Week after week after week she was winning, winning, winning.

The $500 became $1500! That became $2300! A week later she had saved $2850. Within a month she had over $10,000! And still the powerful, uncanny luck didn't dwindle! $20,000, $30,000, $40,000, $50,000, $60,000!

Anna's story is inspiration for housewives everywhere. Today she owns her own home. She doesn't do housework, either! She employs a maid to do that! Anna has become a professional Bingo player, if there is such a thing. When her "inner voice" tells her to, she packs a bag, jets to any city of her choice, stays at fabulous motels, and hits the Bingo parlors and churches. She wins constantly, inevitably!

And what about Ralph S.? How does he employ the mystic secrets of *Psycho-Image Materialization*? Ralph had been working like a slave for years and saving pennies for a spiffy sports car he wanted very much. As the world teaches, that's a wise thing to do—work hard and save your money. As mystic secrets teach, inflation will beat you every time, and you'll be old and decrepit before you realize a single dream. Ralph took steps to short-circuit that kind of life-defeating syndrome.

He practiced the *Psycho-Image Materialization Affirmation* diligently day after day, reworking the hardened soil of his subconscious mind, much like a farmer turns over the soil of his farm to produce bigger and better crops.

Ralph has a little prayer he uses now, which he has shared with me in a letter. I pass it on to you for your use, too. It works best in conjunction with the *Affirmation*, Ralph reports.

> *O Gods of yesterday, O God of now, if I have ever done anything pleasing to you, listen to my heart today and bring me great good fortune. Amen.*

Ralph entered his name in a magazine contest offering a super sports car as first prize. While he waited for the results (*knowing* in advance that he was already the winner and *thanking* the powers for it!) he mentally recited the *Affirmation* and his power-prayer daily. When he saw the big bright envelope in his mail, he could hardly control the rapid beating of his heart. He tore it open and saw with his own eyes the unbelievable: He was the sole winner of the fantastic automobile! $30,000 worth of luxury and fun!

Ralph has since gone on to win all kinds of contests and puzzles by using the secrets of *Psycho-Image Materialization*. Today he's worth approximately $275,000!

What You Should Know About Your Image-Power

Many people talk about the power of the subconscious, but I think you should know how it works. Down through the ages certain mystics and seers have been able to tell us precisely how supernatural forces come to our aid.

As you use *Psycho-Image Materialization Affirmations, Mind Activators, Chants, Prayers, and Spells,* you are, in effect, creating a powerful inner magnet. The more you use the mystic secrets, the stronger your inner magnet.

Once your magnet is powerful enough, it begins to *invisibly* attract to you all that you need, want, wish for, and dream of! According to esoteric knowledge, it works something like this: As you practice subconscious contact through Visualization, your subconscious links with other subconsciouses throughout the universe. This is how Edgar Cayce got in touch with universal medical knowledge—by tapping the Collective Subconscious—other subconsciouses! When this occurs, help and riches and success flow to you—automatically!

An excellent example of this inner, invisible dynamism is Ted G., of Provo, Utah.

How a High School Drop-Out Became a Highly Paid Executive in a Huge Corporation

Ted G. dropped out of high school to help his parents make ends meet. Beginning with that sad necessity, Ted worked for years at common labor, whatever jobs he could find. His parents died many years later and there was Ted, alone, unskilled, and broke.

But this story is about the subconscious. One day, when a forty-year-old Ted was pumping gas in a local station, a wealthy businessman blocks away was thundering at his employees: "I want new creative designs or else! If there aren't some fresh ideas on my desk by morning, some heads are going to roll!"

Here's the connection: Ted was just beginning to employ *Psycho-Image Materialization* secrets to better his lot in this old life. When he started tapping his subconscious, it provided him with great insights, new ideas, and creative artistic impulses. During lunch breaks, he doodled with pen and paper, producing designs.

You guessed it! The powerful subconscious brought these two men together in an uncanny way—*invisibly*!

Ted was wiping the windshield of a glamorous Cadillac, and he heard the rich-looking businessman in the back seat talking about designs. Something came over Ted. He went inside and returned with his designs. Without a word, he passed them through the window to the corporation president. The man took them, looked at them, looked at Ted.

"How much do you make?" he asked.

Ted told him. The man reached inside his jacket and withdrew his wallet. He pulled out two one-hundred dollar bills and gave them to Ted, saying, "Drop that sponge and get in here."

Ted sat in the back seat with the men, and the president said, "Get this man an office. I can see by his work that he doesn't have any equipment to work with. Get him the best! I want these designs on my desk in two hours!"

Now you know how a high school drop-out became an executive in a big corporation at a salary of $45,000 a year!

This is *New Miracle Dynamics IN ACTION!*

What you change in your thoughts changes in your experience! Ted changed his thinking through *Psycho-Image Materialization* secrets and thereby changed his whole life!

Thought is energy, and every time you think, whatever you think about manifests in your daily life. *Psycho-Image Materialization* is your conscious, deliberate use of this dynamic, creative, wonder-working supernatural power.

The Rock-in-the-Pool Image

Have you ever dropped an object—a coin or pebble—into a body of water—a puddle, pond, lake, river, or ocean? What occurs when a solid object hits water?

RIPPLES!

If you drop a rock into a pool of water, ripples immediately fan out and travel ever outward until they wash against the shore, until you behold a series of concentric ever-widening circles.

Think about this Psycho-Image because it is vital to your

understanding the mystic secrets of *Psycho-Image Materialization*. Your thought is the rock; your subconscious mind is the pool of water. When you allow a thought to drop into your subconscious mind, ripples form and spread out. Eventually, they wash up against the shore, that is, they manifest in your outer life!

Anna thought her life should be richer and fuller. The ripples of thought-energy fanned out and manifested in her actual experience, and her life *became* richer and fuller.

Ralph wanted to "short-circuit" the long way around to happiness and possessions. His Psycho-Images rippled his dreams outward, and today his dreams are fully realized!

Ted wanted fun and excitement and riches like other more educated people. *Psycho-Image Materialization* worked a miracle in his life!

It will do the same for you!

The Secret of Transforming Negativity Into Positivity Lies Behind Your Forehead

It is an immutable divine and universal law that what you envision, you attract to yourself. The power of your mind is an awesome thing because it is the physical manifestation of the One Mind—the Source of Supernatural Aid. What the Mind does—creates—you will do with your own mind. The secret to *Psycho-Image Materialization* is the knowledge and awareness of Cause and Effect. What you will do as you absorb the contents of this book is *change the effects by changing the cause*.

Ralph Waldo Emerson said, "Shallow men believe in luck, believe in circumstances: It was somebody's name, or he happened to be there at the time, or it was so then, and another day it would have been otherwise. Strong men believe in cause and effect."[2]

Think about Cause and Effect. Ripples do not form of themselves; they require the rock. Similarly, your outer con-

---

[2]See Theodor Laurence, *The Miracle Power of Believing* (West Nyack, New York: Parker Publishing Company, 1978).

ditions and circumstances have not formed of themselves; they began with your own thoughts. Therefore, if you want to alter your conditions, better your circumstances, change your luck, improve your life in any way—use *Psycho-Image Materialization* as your rock.

Disregard the Effects, Look for the Cause, and Change It!

Do not permit appearances to fool you into defeat, doubt, poverty, ill health, or loneliness. Get right to the *Cause* of things: *Mind*. And know with certainty that as surely as God created the heaven and the earth through His Mind, you can create anything you wish through *your* mind. Your mind and His Mind are one and the same thing! Perhaps you have forgotten this truth. Re-learn it! For this is the key to successful and creative *Psycho-Image Materialization*.

If you have a problem, it is very easy for one to say, "Change your mind and you change your circumstances." The question often asked is: *"How* do I change my mind?" That's where the power of *Psycho-Image Materialization* comes in. By using this technique of mind power you will perform miracles in your own life and rejoice to see all your wishes, dreams and desires come into being.

Janet P. and the Crushing-Eye Psycho-Image

Danger lurked in the corridors of an east San Francisco apartment complex. There was a rapist on the loose. Already five women had been brutally beaten and raped. The police seemed powerless to apprehend the criminal. Janet P. lived alone in an apartment. Week after week came mounting reports of the rapist's activities. There were 23 women living in her apartment building, and when 22 of them had been defiled by the still-free rapist, a reporter asked Janet why she was not afraid. Janet had no desire to expose her secrets, but she said: "I am divinely protected." That is all she would say.

What she did not tell the inquiring man is that she practices *Psycho-Image Materialization* daily. When the threat of physical rape became all too real, she began using a particular Psycho-Image.

One night, at a few minutes to midnight, Janet heard a noise outside her bedroom window. She jolted herself awake and turned on the lamp just as a hooded man leapt into her room.

Janet sat up and stared straight at the man, a powerfully built person, obviously intent upon doing her bodily harm. This man had already enjoyed absolute freedom during his evil acts. He was now confident that this lovely woman before him would be his next victim. But a strange and frightening thing happened—to *him*!

He was suddenly gripped with intense pains in his groin, so intense that he had to double over and grab his stomach. It felt as if someone were kicking him in the belly. Then an excruciating pain ripped through his head, dazing him, making his mind spin, twisting his head on his shoulders. Then, what felt like a huge weight came crashing down on top of his skull.

The man fell to the floor, twisting and writhing, crying out in pain, suffering unseen agonies.

Janet P. was sitting quietly in her bed, staring. What was she doing? She was using the Crushing-Eye Psycho-Image! This powerful Image can be used by you, too—not only to thwart a rapist, but to end any kind of oppression, to discourage any kind of enemy, to conquer any kind of threat! What Janet accomplished with this secret power, you can accomplish anywhere and anytime you wish! Here's the power Image.

New Miracle Dynamics Mind Activator #1

Picture It! You are a living channel for Higher Forces. Like a prism reflecting white light into seven colors, you are a human prism beaming seven Powers of Might, Safety, Defense, Wrath, Fire, Destruction, and Annihilation.

Above you, in the Invisible Realm, is the powerful Eye of God, like an intense beam of radiant Light infusing you with Divine Energy. It looks through your eyes at what threatens you—and what threatens you is *annihilated*! This is why Janet was staring at the rapist and why he was suddenly and supernaturally attacked by Higher Forces that will tolerate no evil, that will *punish* evil for you!

Janet did not let the "appearance" of evil frighten or subdue her. She became a prism for Supreme Powers. Evil was erased from her life instantly, powerfully, automatically!

> *The enemy said I will pursue, I will overtake, I will divide the spoil; my lust shall be satisfied upon them; I will draw my sword, my hand shall destroy them.*
>
> *Thou didst blow with thy wind, the sea covered them: they sank as lead in the mighty waters.*
>
> *Who is like unto thee, O Lord, among the gods? who is like thee, glorious in holiness, fearful in praises, doing wonders?*
>
> *Thou stretchedst out thy right hand, the earth swallowed them.*
>
> *Thou in thy mercy hast led forth the people which thou hast redeemed: thou hast guided them in thy strength unto thy holy habitation.*
>
> Exodus 15:9-13

If You Know What You Want, Nothing Is Stopping You from Obtaining It

Know what you want. Get a clear mental picture of your need or desire and *hold onto it*. COMPLETELY ENJOY this Psycho-Imaging of health, wealth, love, or whatever you choose. Then, when you can feel the exhilaration of success—STOP! Let go of the Psycho-Image. It has already passed into your subconscious mind and needs no further aid. Remember: your Psycho-Image is the rock you are dropping into the pool of your subconscious mind. We don't "push" a rock into water, do we? We simply let it drop, and then it is out of our hands. By the same token, when you consciously and deliberately use a Psycho-Image, you let it "drop" into your subconscious mind and LET GO! Your all-powerful subconscious will do the rest. In fact, if you worry about it or continue to hold it after the feeling of joy and accomplishment, you will *cancel* it! I cannot begin to tell you of the hundreds of people who practice mind power techniques this *wrong* way: even though they have dropped the "rock" of positive thinking into their subconscious "pool," they continue to worry it, wonder if it will work, even try adding another, larger "rock." And then they wonder why they are not getting results! These miracles are not done by will power, but by God-power, by the mystic secret of *Psycho-Image Materialization*, which is: LET GO AND LET GOD.

Picture your desire; envision it strongly; desire it hotly, see yourself getting it in your mind's eye; realize that your desire is coming to you right at that moment; then LET GO OF IT! If you can, forget about it completely, knowing that on the invisible plane of existence your desire is taking on concrete form for you. What you have desired and empowered with *Psycho-Image Materialization* will come into your life shortly!

New Miracle Dynamics Works to the Degree That You Disregard Appearances

As you practice *Psycho-Image Materialization*, *believe* you are going to see positive, rewarding results. Do *not* let appearances fool you, discourage you, sway you, or interrupt your *Psycho-Image Materialization* exercises. Remember: What Mind is manifesting may take some time. It is for you to believe without seeing that what you want *is*!

Your new bywords are these: St. Paul said, "We walk by

faith, not by sight." And St. Augustine said, "Faith is to believe what we do not see; and the reward of this faith is to see what we believe."

This, in a nutshell, is the principle behind *Psycho-Image Materialization*. In spite of conditions, circumstances or physical appearances without, you will believe implicitly that *within* all is perfect, that your Psycho-Images *will* manifest on this material plane.

Do this and nothing will be denied you!

Valuable Tips You Will Want to Remember

Throughout this book, use Chapter 1 as your guide. It is the chapter that cultivates your mind so you can reap a harvest of riches from the remaining chapters. For example:

1. Get alone with yourself and relax according to instructions in this chapter.
2. *Always* bear in mind that you are communicating subconsciously with a Divine Agency above and beyond your finite mind. Recognize the One Mind as the One Source of all the good things you are receiving.
3. Practice *Psycho-Image Materialization Affirmation #1* daily. Some people find it wise to recite (orally or mentally) this Affirmation before using those in succeeding chapters—somewhat of a mind-preparation Affirmation.
4. When you Psycho-Image, do so BIG! The bigger your mental picture, the more charged it is with your desire or emotion, the greater are the chances of it—or something remarkably like it—materializing in your experience.
5. By all means, be *thankful*! Do not wait for results before you give thanks for your blessings. *Gratitude prior to receipt* is a metaphysical law that *guarantees* results. Remember that Jesus thanked his Father for the raising of Lazarus *before* it occurred—and then Lazarus came forth!

6. You possess the power! For your mind and Infinite Mind are one and same thing! You have been using this power all your life, but now you will DIRECT it!

7. Remember the Rock-in-the-Pool Image: Drop your need or desire into your subconscious mind and LET GO! God, Mind, Infinite Intelligence will do the rest. Given the proper impetus, your thought will send out ripples of energy, and that thought will materialize in your life.

8. Above all, *disregard effects, look for the cause, and change it!* Always remember that the *cause* is always in the mind, inside, not outside, within, not without. Change the inner, and you change the outer!

9. Practice *New Miracle Dynamics Activator #1.* Know that like the unassailable butterfly, you are divinely protected from the negative effects of conditions and circumstances. Then practice *all* the Psycho-Images provided for you throughout this book. Chapter 1 prepares you and your mind to reap a harvest of riches from the other chapters.

10. Take each chapter as it comes, follow its instructions, practice its techniques. In short: Psycho-Image and go forth conquering, gaining, succeeding, exhilarating, WINNING!

11. Most importantly, rest in the knowledge that as you carry out the dynamic instructions throughout this book, you are actually activating invisible and supernatural aid from other universes. By practicing the *Psycho-Image Materialization Affirmations* and the *New Miracle Dynamics Mind Activators*, you are making subliminal contact with these powerful, higher-than-human agencies that in turn, will come to your aid, do your bidding, serve you, support you, sustain you. All you have to do then is sit back, relax, and reap the joyful benefits!

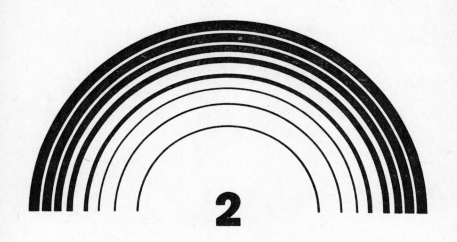

2

Obtain and Pyramid Mountains of Money Through Psycho-Image Materialization

If you will be needing money—if you need money *now*—the proper/powerful use of *Psycho-Image Materialization* will bring it to you!

But, as always, *first things first*. If you believe for any reason that money is the root of all evil, perish the thought. Get your mind clear of this energy short-circuit! St. Paul did not say that money is the root of all evil; he said that "the *love* of money is the root of all evil" (I Timothy 6:10). The inordinate *love* of money is the dangerous belief that money is the *answer* to all our problems. It is not. The solution to our problems is that which *brings* money, as well as all other good things: the Universal Mind.

What You Should Know About Money—
Why You Don't Have It and How to Get
All You Need

Remember our premise: Mind is All, gives birth to All, provides All. If All is given to us by God (Infinite Intelligence, Mind, Spirit), then *money*, too, is such a gift and, like all else manifesting in this material world, it is *good*. It is wise to remember that men and women who have an inordinate love of money—though they have none—are often the source of evil. Think of the man who robs the local liquor store or bank. What makes him steal? The *love* of money, the erroneous belief that money will cure his ills. Obviously, if the possession of money is the root of all evil, *all* poor people would be extremely good people, even the bank robber! No, the possession of money is not evil; it is good—especially if you know where money comes from!

Money is an effect, not a cause. Anything that does not create itself is effect. And the power behind every effect is the One Cause—Mind. Through the use of *Psycho-Image Materialization* you penetrate the veil of effect and get right to the Cause, the Producer of All good things in your life.

Through *Psycho-Image Materialization*, you create your own "money consciousness." Consciousness is Cause (as you think, so you are) and when you create your money-consciousness, you *make* money appear in your physical life. Those who are not conscious of money as an effect do not have money; those who *are* so conscious have mountains of money! If you understand and believe (or better yet, *know*) that Divine Law governs your life at all times, spiritually and materially, money cannot be kept from you.

Begin right this minute to start the money flowing into your life by practicing the following mystic key to wealth and riches:

Psycho-Image Materialization Affirmation #2

The Power that created me is the Power of Perfection. My present wealth is the consequence of the perfect action of this Almighty Power, and I am grateful for what I have. I joyously permit thoughts of greater wealth and riches to circulate through my mind. These ideas are centers and magnets for my incoming money, gifts, and supply. This powerful Psycho-Image is my key to increased abundance.

Any and all appearances of lack and deprivation in my consciousness are now cast out like demons and are abolished forever from my thoughts. All patterns of great wealth are now activated and permeate my every waking thought. They attract money and all the good things of life to me.

I appreciate the wealth that I now have and the increase of this wealth that I shall have. I open now to the Divine influx of wealth that shall appear in my experience as money. I know that it is done unto me according to my belief, and I

> believe totally in this miraculous influx of wealth. Perfect Power is my Source of Riches. And so it is!

How Bill M. Turned His Abject Poverty into Glorious Riches Through Psycho-Image Materialization

Bill M., of Topeka, Kansas, had problems that are today so prevalent that one would think it is predestination for us to experience lack and privation. Bill's creditors were hounding him, threatening him with repossession of his car, his furniture, even his typewriter. His children, a little boy and girl, were beginning to go hungry. His wife was growing ill with worry and anxiety.

"What am I going to do?" Bill cried in anguish. "I didn't expect to get laid off from my job. I'm not prepared for it. Are we going to lose our home? Where will we live? What will we eat? I don't want to go on welfare or get food stamps. I've always been independent and self-sufficient. I want to stay that way. But how can I when poverty stalks us day in and day out? Things are getting worse, not better."

The biggest mistake Bill could make was to entertain these thoughts in his mind. He was permitting false appearances to sow doubt in his mind. He had to get back in touch with what Franklin Delano Roosevelt meant when he said: "The only limit to our realizations of tomorrow will be our doubts of today." Bill wanted to realize wealth, health, and security, but no one can realize such blessings so long as he or she permits success-defeating doubts to act like parasites in the mind. If Bill had continued in this mode of thinking, there is no doubt that things would indeed have gotten worse instead of better for him. But he did not pursue this perilous course.

He took up *New Miracle Dynamics*. He renewed his faith in things unseen, believing that what was not yet seen would inexorably appear if only he held on to his faith. The end could have been complete disaster and misery if his doubt reigned supreme in his mind. "If the Sun and Moon should doubt," said the incomparable William Blake, "they'd immediately go out." And so it is with us human beings. The Light of our lives goes out when we doubt Divine Law and its inexorable ability to form in our material lives the very things we believe are ours. And so it would have been with Bill had he not learned about *Psycho-Image Materialization* and *used* it—undoubtingly!

Do you need money? Are your bills accumulating? How about some money just for fun and leisure and pleasure? How would you like cash to flow to you—*inevitably*? Yes—inevitably!

Here is the *Mind Activator* that Bill used to create amazing results and happy monetary conditions in his life:

---

new Miracle Dynamics Mind Activator #2

Imagine yourself as possessing the "mind of Christ," that is, the consciousness that no matter what you ask, Supreme Intelligence will respond positively. In mind and in a spirit of gratitude, ask for wealth—not money, which is the outer expression of spiritual Wealth. Ask for GREAT WEALTH! See yourself open to an influx of pouring, cascading, overwhelming Wealth— more wealth than you can conceive! See yourself reposed, receptive, unstriving, unworried— simply an irrepressible magnet for wealth. In this state of mind, money will flow to you— inevitably!

A man brings about real increase by producing in himself the conditions for it, that is, through receptivity to and love of the good. Thus the thing for which he strives comes of itself, with the inevitability of natural law.

> *Where increase is thus in harmony with the highest laws of the universe, it cannot be prevented by any constellation of accidents.*
>
> I Ching

How He Did It

Through the creative use of *Psycho-Image Materialization*, Bill M. won a brand new automobile through a Sweepstakes. He then *gave* his old car back to the people who were threatening to repossess it—with a great deal of personal satisfaction! Through *Psycho-Image Materialization*, he obtained a houseful of furniture. Food literally bulges the cupboards of his happy home. His wife is extremely happy, healthy, and joyous. What Bill did to completely reverse "obvious" negativity, you can do, too. Bill employed a three-step program for himself, like this:

1. He prepared his troubled mind by getting alone with himself and reciting *Psycho-Image Materialization Affirmation #2*. Bill says he spoke it aloud into his subconscious mind three times and then, with eyes closed in peaceful repose, said it to himself mentally over and over, concentrating only on preparing the "soil of the mind" to receive abundance and goodness.

2. He followed this preparatory procedure by contemplating and meditating upon *Mind Activator #2*. This meditation opened his mind to receiving the help he needed and desired. After practicing this *Psycho-Image Materialization* five times, he knew that *nothing*—appearances notwithstanding—could possibly block his eventual good!

3. So believing, Bill then proceeded to employ his own *Psycho-Image Materialization* powers by Psycho-Imaging what he wanted. Bill explains:

"My head was really mixed up when I began, all clogged with worries and doubts. But after the very first recital of the AFFIRMATION, something started happening to me, in my mind, my spirit. I began to feel release from pressure and anxiety. By the time I finished saying it, I felt like a living magnet for all kinds of wealth and happiness.

"The second stage—the *Mind Activator*—also had a profound effect on me. I found my sense of doubt and unbelief just falling away like so many leaves from a tree. I was able to sit there in perfect confidence and conviction that all would be well. That one line: 'Thus the thing for which he strives comes of itself, with the inevitability of natural law,' really hit home with me. I *knew* in my heart that nothing could be denied me now.

"That made the third stage easy, fun, and exciting. I started my own Psycho-Imaging."

Our Needs and Circumstances Are Different, But You Can Use the Same New Miracle Dynamics Technique that Bill M. Used

Your individual needs and desires tell you what to Psycho-Image during your *Psycho-Image Materialization* practices. Bill's "mental pictures" are appended here to (1) show you how he changed poverty into wealth and (2) to illustrate the way you will use your own creative imagination for yourself.

You will remember that Bill was being threatened by bill collectors. His car was going to be repossessed. This worried him a great deal, of course, but only until he used the *Affirmation* and *Mind Activator #2*. Then he was able to utilize his innate, God-given power to change conditions and circumstances in his own life. Bill says:

"I knew there was a Sweepstakes on offering a brand new car, but I've never bothered with such things until now. This time I felt I could Psycho-

Image to *make* that car mine. I imagined it as already done! I thanked God for that car long before I owned it! I saw myself going up to the man in charge of the operation. I saw myself receiving the keys to the car from his hand. I saw the people gathered round, amazed that I'd won such a fabulous prize. I pictured myself driving out of the showroom in my brand new, sparkling automobile. I saw my kids and my wife laughing for joy. And, by God, it worked!

"Three days later a phone call informed me that I was the winner of the car! I took my wife with me to claim it. I let her drive it first. I wanted the pleasure of driving my old car downtown to the hardhearted creditors and turning it over to them. Boy, were they shocked! They were in the business of repossessing cars, but they'd never had a laughing man drive it in himself!"

Where did Bill's furniture come from? He used *Psycho-Image Materialization* to "picture" his home filled with his own furniture, without payments due. Even his wife was dubious about this request, but Bill was adamant. He practiced *Psycho-Image Materialization Affirmation #2*, reread and reabsorbed the power of *Mind Activator #2*, and then Psycho-Imaged what he desired—no matter how incredible it seemed.

Bill says: "I found out one thing important. What you Psycho-Image in your mind doesn't always occur exactly how you pictured it."

This *is* important. You may Psycho-Image yourself buying a fur coat or a yacht, but in actual experience, the thing you want may be *given* to you or you may *win* it or come by it in any number of ways. You may not *buy* it.

Bill learned this when a man came to his door a few days after he had won the car. This man, Ernie B., was the owner of a local furniture manufacturing business. His newspaper ads always had the slogan: "The Lucky Family Has Ernie's Suites." He came to Bill to ask him a favor. He said: "I see in the paper that you won the Sweepstakes. What I'd like to do is capitalize on your phenomenal luck. I'd like to advertise you as one of the 'Lucky Families' that use only my furniture. What I'll do is completely furnish your home for you if you will permit photographers to come in and take pictures of it and your family enjoying it."

Of course Bill agreed immediately and signed the agreement. This was his answer to *Psycho-Image Materialization* practices! Delightfully for Bill, Ernie threw in a spanking new electric typewriter, which alone is worth $500!

What about all that food in the cupboards? Well, in a sense it came about through *Psycho-Image Materialization*. As Bill puts it: "Heck, all this luck left me some money that no longer had to go into bill collectors' pockets. I took my wife and kids on a spree through the grocery store! We're having steak tonight!"

His wife's recovery of health and vitality was a natural—but wondrous!—consequence of his new way of thought. Bill, his wife, and his children are paradisiacally happy today, using *Psycho-Image Materialization* for whatever need comes up. "And not only needs," Bill writes enthusiastically. "We use it for fun, too!"

What Bill M. Has, You Can Have— and More!

Please take careful note of the chain-reaction effect of *Psycho-Image Materialization*. As you can see in Bill's case, once you activate your dormant receiving powers, link upon link of wealth, goodness, and happiness occurs. One thing leads to another—inexorably! In amazing, sometimes startling ways, you simply accumulate wealth from all sides. Be ready for this!

Follow Bill's procedures:

1. Ingest into your subconscious mind the fertilizing *Psycho-Image Materialization Affirmation*.

2. Quietly and *believingly* practice *Mind Activator #2*,

opening yourself to receive all that you hope for, wish for, desire, need, or dream of!

3. Activate your own power of creative imagination: visualize yourself *in detail* receiving precisely what you want out of life here and now. Entertain variations on the theme. For example, if you are looking for a job, picture yourself going to get it, being informed of a good job by phone, "falling into" a fantastic job by meeting a stranger who turns out to be your boss. This kind of *Psycho-Image Materialization attracts* to you exactly what you need!

Remember: What you desire may come to you in totally unexpected and delightful ways once you open yourself through *Psycho-Image Materialization*. Expect the unexpected!

The Secret of Psycho-Image Materialization Is Yours to Use and Enjoy

The secret mechanism—at once psychological and spiritual—that Bill M. and other users of *Psycho-Image Materialization* have discovered and benefited from is this: *In psychospiritual realms, like attracts like.*

As you probably know, in the physical realm, opposites attract. Perish this thought when dealing with Mind Power. It is unthinkable! It would mean that the saint attains Godhood by contemplating the Devil! It would mean a man or a woman obtains love by harboring thoughts of hatred!

When employing the wonder-working power of *Psycho-Image Materialization* always remember that *like attracts like!* In other words, what you Psycho-Image in your mind is what you attract to yourself in experience! The thought of lack attracts poverty! The thought of destitution attracts lack! The thought of "no money" empties your pockets, your bank account, your life! Use *Psycho-Image Materialization to increase* your money, *multiply* your wealth, *magnify* your life. You do this by getting into the proper frame of mind (use the *Psycho-Image Materialization Affirmations* and the *Mind Activators* provided for you), and by Psycho-Imaging in glorious color and with deep feeling what you want! Others are doing so right now. So can you!

How Psycho-Image Materialization Transforms Lack into Plenty, Poverty into Riches, Dearth into Wealth

When you prepare your subconscious mind through the use of *Psycho-Image Materialization Affirmations* and *Mind Activators*, you are in essence directing your creative wellspring to supply you with whatever you mentally picture. Inexorable, immutable, and universal Law does the work. Your subconscious mind cannot pick and choose for you: it gives you whatever you are imagining in your mind, whatever you are feeling strongly, whatever you are desiring ardently. Knowing this key to cause and effect, you are now in the enviable position of mastering your life, your conditions, your circumstances. You can now drop the right kind of rock into the pool of your subconscious mind—and watch riches ripple into your experience! Do you want more money? Then PSYCHO-IMAGE it!

Joan L. Psycho-Imaged Herself Getting a Raise and Received a Miracle

Just two dollars more an hour. That's all Joan L. of Lancaster, Pennsylvania asked for. As a secretary in one company for over two years, she justifiably felt she deserved this raise. She practiced *Psycho-Image Materialization*, mentally recited *Psycho-Image Materialization Affirmation #2*, and then went to her employer and asked for the raise. The man, much older than Joan, who is 22, immediately and suggestively asked for a date with her. "Let's talk it over at dinner this evening," he said. Joan was dismayed and returned to her desk disturbed. She saw the situation right away: if she refused his desire, she could not only lose the raise but her job as well! A lesser woman would have been totally unnerved by this kind of behavior. (This situation, by the way, is one that is shared by many working women today). Joan went back to her desk in the outer office and, appearances notwithstanding, repeated her *Psycho-Image Materialization* exercises. She mentally repeated *Psycho-Image Materialization Affirmation #2*, reinforced her conviction of Truth with *New Miracle Dynamics Mind Activator #2*, and reviewed her own Psycho-Image of herself receiving the raise she wanted—regardless of her employer's behavior! The day wore on and five o'clock was approaching, the time she was expected to make her answer to the boss, the time any other woman would consider a grave crisis. But Joan continued in her faith. At ten minutes to five a late client came in, a young man from an important company, and he asked to see the president. Joan was busily using the intercom when the young man narrowed his eyes on the nameplate on her desk.

"I've seen your name on letters," he said with a nice smile. "So you're his right-hand-woman, huh? I've never seen such neat work." And he added jokingly: "Maybe I'll steal you from him."

He went inside with the boss and conducted business for about fifteen minutes. But more than that transpired, apparently. Perhaps the boss proudly aired his conviction that this evening he was going to ravish his secretary. At any rate, the young man emerged from the office, went over to Joan, and said: "Think me forward if you want, but I don't think this is the place for a woman like yourself. I don't think he appreciates you for what you truly are. Here's my card. I'll leave it up to you. If you wish to, you can start work on Monday morning as my personal secretary."

He left without another word. Joan's heart was beating like a tom-tom. She needed no further "sign" that her *Psycho-Image Materialization* was manifesting itself miraculously. When her employer appeared, ready to snare his prize, she coolly brushed by him, leaving him standing there with his mouth agape in surprise. On Monday morning she began work in a plush new office with a man who respected her ability, at *twice* the salary she had been receiving!

Joan had asked for two dollars and received a miracle!

This is precisely how *Psycho-Image Materialization* will work in your life as you attune yourself to the indefatigable Source of All.

How Carter P. Turned an Idle Wish into Exciting Reality

Carter P., of Cincinnati, Ohio, is a cabdriver—but not the run-of-the-mill cabdriver. Not any more! He once had been. Slaving away for a weekly (and weak!) paycheck, he dreamed of someday being able to go on a South Pacific cruise—a big dream for an overworked, underpaid cabbie. He turned this "idle daydreaming" into creative imagination through the use of *Psycho-Image Materialization*. Throughout the long hours of driving others to their important destinations, he practiced the vitalizing technique: *Psycho-Image Materialization Affirmation* and *New Miracle Dynamics Mind Activator #2*. And he Psycho-Imaged himself sunning on a pleasant beach beneath blue sky beside unpolluted surf. Having thus prepared his subconscious mind for Divine influx of goodness, strange and marvelous things began to happen in his life. For one thing, he won a magazine contest that offered exactly the cruise he had been dreaming about earlier. But that wasn't the end of Carter's new abundance. He met a young woman on the golden beach one day, and it became a habit for them to meet every afternoon after lunch. They just sat and talked; the young woman apparently needed someone to talk to. She often told him she had no one with whom she could "relate."

It wasn't long before Carter found himself falling in love with her. Finally, he told her so. Later he talked of marriage. The woman was evasive, hesitant. She asked him if he would still love her if he found out she were something other than he thought. Carter did not understand this mysterious talk, but said: "I'd love you and want to marry you no matter what." That was what the young woman wanted to hear. She consented to marry him, to introduce him to her parents, etc. That's when Carter received the shock of his life. Her father is one of the wealthiest tycoons in the islands! He soon discovered that his love's "mysteriousness" centered around the fact that most of her life she has been pursued by men who were after her money and not her for herself. In Carter she found a simple, earthy young man who loved her.

They married. Today, between trips to the islands, Carter still drives a cab—but with one big difference! His happy father-in-law *bought* the taxi company and gave it to Carter as a wedding present! Carter now laughingly says: "I just drive around two or three hours a day, when I feel like it, usually in the nicest weather." He's now his own man. At night he goes home like other cabdrivers, but not to the room he used to live in, but to the largest richest sprawling home in the wealthiest part of town. Summers, he and his wife go to their private ski resort in Colorado. Winters, they vacation in the islands, sometimes on the Riviera, sometimes at other exotic places around the globe.

Carter *Psycho-Imaged* and opened the floodgates of Divine influx! He held onto a dream and permitted it to manifest itself in its own way. He wanted one thing and received a thousand! His life is still rippling with joy.

You can do the same! Prepare your subconscious mind through the dynamic use of *Psycho-Image Affirmations* and *Psycho-Image Mind Activators*, dream your dreams in living color, and let go! Visualize what you want—dream BIG!—and let the Power of this Universe supply you with what you desire! *It* will do so—if you will let *It*!

How Psycho-Image Materialization Lifted a Man out of Poverty and Lack

Herman T., of Louisville, Kentucky, at age 62 had been a janitor for over twenty years. Because of his advanced years, Herman was laid off and suddenly found himself among the growing number of idle senior citizens. He was lost, losing his money daily through heavy debts, bills, and obligations. Life seemed to be deserting him. But he tried to find work. "I looked everywhere," he says. "No one would give me so much as a chance because of my age. They wanted to put me out to pasture. That's when I heard about *Psycho-Image Materialization*, and I tried it. I'd already tried everything else."

Like many, many older people who cannot survive on Social Security, Herman only asked for the opportunity to help himself, to work with dignity, to be a living and vital part of some company. He practiced *Psycho-Image Materialization Affirmation #2* and *New Miracle Dynamics Mind Activator #2*. Then he Psycho-Imaged himself being hired as a custodian of a big apartment complex. This was all he asked—a simple job to support himself. But this is *not* what he obtained. When he applied for the position and learned it was already filled, he continued to use this Psycho-Image *anyway*, undaunted by *appearances*. It does not matter how you Psycho-Image yourself increasing your wealth; it is only important that you *do* so, that you bravely drop the rock of positive thought into the pool of your subconscious mind.

Herman had been practicing *Psycho-Image Materialization* for ten days when the miracle occurred. He received a phone call from a new firm in town that had heard about him when it canvassed the city for help. Herman was asked to come to the personnel office for interview. He was overjoyed. As far as he was concerned his *Psycho-Image Materialization* had paid off; he had found work. But there was more to it than that.

During his interview, Herman discovered that this was a new janitorial company planning to open and operate a huge series of janitorial service companies. Upon hearing this, Herman was simply further convinced that he had found a job. But then the personnel director dropped the bombshell. "What we are asking of you," he said, "is your willingness to manage these companies for us." Herman was astounded!

Today he manages a string of fifty such companies, driving around in a company-provided, company-maintained Cadillac, and his salary is not $3.00 per hour—but $36,000 per-year!

Money Is the Physical Manifestation of Spiritual Wealth—and Psycho-Image Materialization Influences the Spiritual Realm

Wealth is more an energy, a Divine energy, than anything else: a flow of power, if you will. Money is the concrete expression of wealth. We cannot control a flow of money; but we *can* influence the flow of wealth, which will then manifest as money in our experience. *Psycho-Image Materialization* is your private key to this influencing of wealth-flow. Learn to use it daily, wisely, with enthusiasm and expectation. Your Psycho-Images will attract *like*. Some people receive exactly what they "picture," the way they picture it; others receive far more than they pictured and in ways they hardly expected!

A Pennsylvania woman named Alice D. Psycho-Imaged her husband into a fantastic pay raise! Through the powerful use of *Psycho-Image Materialization*, she pictured her husband Fred receiving a gigantic pay raise so they could pay their bills and have some fun out of life, too. Just one week later Fred was summoned to the boss's office. He was told that he had been chosen for a new job opening "upstairs," meaning a better position and better money! Today Fred takes home $2700 more a year than ever before!

Know What You Want and Go After It

Before practicing *Psycho-Image Materialization*, make a list of the ten things that would please you tremendously. Your "shopping list" might look like this:

I want the following things:

1. A rewarding, exciting job, with a fabulous salary.
2. Contest winnings of more than $1000.
3. A sparkling, kind, and rich mate.
4. A fantastic vacation trip of fun and luxury.
5. Power over my enemies.
6. My very own business, both exciting and profitable.
7. Enduring love and lasting marriage with the man (woman) of my choice.
8. A powerful personality, amazing charisma, and magnetic attraction for the opposite sex.
9. Psychic gifts, spiritual powers, supernatural aid.

10. Innumerable friends, great social life, happiness, and
endless fun activity.

Others Are Getting What They Want: So Can You!

Mary B., of Bronx, New York, wanted some extra
money just for the fun of it. She and her young husband were
barely managing on his meager salary. Mary couldn't take a
job, as she lives confined to a wheelchair. But one day she was
on the front porch, setting a pot of flowers into a yarn holder
she had marcaméd. A passing woman saw it and asked her if
she would sell it; it was beautiful. She gave Mary $25 for it!
Today, Mary enjoys her "hobby" more than ever, for suddenly people from all over want to purchase her beautiful
flower pots that she creates in macramé. In one month alone,
Mary joyfully reports, she has made as much as $900!

She Psycho-Imaged herself getting money in defiance of
all appearances that said she couldn't possibly receive
additional income—and her Psycho-Image attracted *like*.

Ella C., of Atlanta, Georgia, Psycho-Imaged herself receiving a check for $1,000,000. This is thinking big! She did
not receive a million dollars. But her heartfelt Psycho-Image
sent out strong ripples of need. Consequently, she won a
contest for $10,000—and that's "nothing to sneeze at," as Ella
now says.

Fred T., of San Diego, California, needed money for his
hospital bills. He was desperate and in despair. Though he
had practiced *Psycho-Image Materialization* as outlined in
this book, he still lost faith because things weren't happening
fast enough to suit him. One day he determined to end it
all—yes, to commit suicide, to take his own life. He took an
old gun he owned and drove to a secluded area of town to do
this deed. He chose a garbage dump "because I felt like garbage," as he says. Crying bitterly he held the gun to his head
and, looking down as he said his goodbyes to a cruel world, he
saw something through his tear-filled eyes. He wiped his eyes
and bent down—and found a metal container with over
$50,000 in it! By law, the money is his if no one claims it. It is

now in his bank account, still a mystery as to where it came from.

You can see the necessity of unflagging faith here: Fred might have pulled the trigger before his subconscious even had the chance to respond to his needs! What a tragedy that would have been! But there is no tragedy in Fred's life now; there is nothing but happiness and laughter and a great deal of healthy, wholesome fun and excitement.

The New Miracle Dynamics Secret that Insures Your Receipt of Greater Riches

1. In your quiet place, mentally and/or orally say *Psycho-Image Materialization Affirmation #2.*

2. Once your subconscious mind is turned away from appearances of discord, mentally and/or orally recite *New Miracle Dynamics Mind Activator #2.*

3. You are now in the frame of mind necessary for manifesting invisible wealth as visible money in your personal experience. Still in this magical consciousness, begin your Psycho-Imaging. See yourself as solving all your money problems. See how money is being given to you, arriving, coming through the mail, or whatever—but see yourself receiving mountains of money, great amounts of money. See yourself using this money, enjoying it, spreading cheer and goodwill with it.

4. This *Psycho-Image Materialization* technique is infallible for fertilizing the soil of your receptive subconscious mind and for preparing you to receive your heart's desire. Psycho-Image frequently and with *feeling.*

5. *Rake in your riches!* You can see how easy it really is once you fertilize your subconscious mind with *Psycho-Image Materialization Affirmations* and *New Miracle Dynamics Mind Activators*—all you have to do then is sit back and let your new-found

wealth come pouring into your life! Relax in the comfort of your own home, do not move a finger, do not worry or doubt, just relax, receive, and enjoy. The Great Materializer will do all the work *for* you!

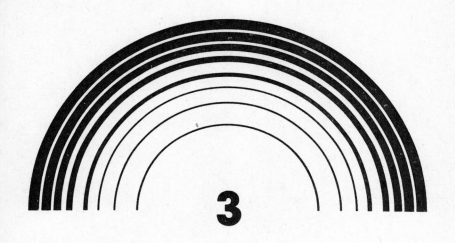

3

How to Use
The Psycho-Image Materialization
Key to Miraculous Healing

Health is not something you have or possess; health is something you *are*.

Contemplate this statement. Think about it for a few moments, for it is the key to healthy vigor and vitality. If you believe health is something you can lose, then of course it can be lost. If, however, you come into the secret mystic knowledge that you *are* health, it cannot be lost. Do you see what I'm getting at? *As you believe, so you receive!*

Ann P., of Indianapolis, Indiana, believed she had lost the sight in one eye. Doctors told her so. Facts spoke for themselves. But mystic truth and objective facts are not always the same thing. Incredibly, remarkably, time and again, doctors are astounded when some little known mystical truth restores health to a person supposedly ill, diseased, or crippled. Ann P.'s case was not really hopeless. Nor was that of James L., of Los Angeles, California, nor that of Edna M., of Greenfield, Massachusetts. These fortunate people (and many more like them) have discovered for themselves that medical facts are not always the last word on illness. They discovered this by discovering themselves, by unearthing from within themselves vast reservoirs of miracle-healing powers. And what they did, *you* can do! You begin by revaluating what you have been taught about health.

If You Do Not Know the Source of Health, You Can Lose It; if You Know the Source of Health, You Can *Never* Lose It!

Let's clear the slate. Pills are not the key to health (Ann P. threw pills away forever when she learned the secret of Psycho-Image Materialization!). Surgery is not always the answer either (many people have escaped the ordeal and cost of surgery through self-realization techniques!). Simply stated: The key to your health is rarely external. It is usually internal. Even doctors must admit that though they do their best to "cure" a patient, it is ultimately that person's faith in themselves and their desire to live that pulls them through. In short, it is inner power and not outer expertise that really provides health.

Let's get on the right track about health, the secret mystic track. I have discussed this subject with many people across the country, some of whom have joyfully experienced so-called miraculous healings, and a consensus of their opinions, feelings, and beliefs comes to this: Health is a dynamic movement of inner energy, as much a part of you as your breathing, heartbeat, or pulse. Health is not something you get or lose. Health is the joyous activity of life-energy moving in, through, and around you. Taking the eyes and mind away from this truth and looking outside for cure-alls causes blockages that result in disease. Disease (dis-ease) occurs when we are not at ease with ourselves, when we are cut off from certain metaphysical truths about our being, when we forget that health is a movement within us, sustaining us, invigorating us, maintaining our organisms. You can see the principle of energy-movement when you consider the river. From its inception in the mountains, the river carries nutriments and soil and moves them across the land, irrigating and vitalizing everything it touches. It does this without question, without hesitation, naturally—the way we should be channeling flowing, energizing health.

Let us now compare the river with you. Your subconscious mind is the river that, when flowing freely, distributes life-giving, life-sustaining energies throughout your body. As you become one with your metaphysical source of health, you automatically dissolve obstacles to perfect health, and you permit a freer flow of invigorating energy. But how do you un-dam this important river of health?

The Psycho-Image Secret to Health, Vigor, and Vitality

There are a few steps you can take immediately to bring ill health to a screeching halt. If you are concerned about a loved one, a friend, or an acquaintance who needs fast and effective help, simply bear that person in mind when following these simple rules:

1. Get alone with yourself. Take a few deep breaths, just to put yourself in a more relaxed and receptive attitude.

2. Clear your mind of all extraneous thoughts. One Psycho-Image technique is to mentally picture yourself standing before a blackboard. Lift the eraser and clear the slate of all writing. Imagine the slate to be your mind. This "Psycho-Imaging" will, in effect, clear your mind, for your Psycho-Image Materialization exercise.

3. Prepare yourself to receive and acknowledge metaphysical aid. Thus prepared, read aloud or say mentally the following seed-affirmation.

Psycho-Image Materialization Affirmation #3

I am serene in the presence of the Great Physician who heals all and sustains all in perfect health. He is the epitome of perfection in Mind, Word, and Spirit; as His image and likeness, I am perfect health in mind, body, and soul. This eternal healing Presence flows to me, through me, and out of me to others, leaving me healthy, whole, energetic, alive, and exuberant. From the top of my head to the bottom of my feet, I am afloat in a warm sea of healing fluid. An influx of divine health fills me, permeates me, animates me. There is nothing in me to deny this truth; therefore there is no spot or blemish in my physical body. In truth, my physical body and my spiritual body are one, and as the spiritual is perfect and whole, so is the physical. I now claim this truth as my own, and I am uni-

fied with the perfect God, the Great Physician. My blood transports healing substance to every corner of my body. I breathe in health and breathe out dis-ease. My inner organs operate in harmony, each performing its function properly, in order, and without hindrance. My vitality increases, my eyes light up, my heart beats with joyous response.

As this remarkable health and energy heals me and keeps me whole, it emanates to all around me and heals each. In praise and thanksgiving, I accept my wholeness and perfection and the wholeness and perfection of everyone around me.

No one is healthier than I am; no one is less healthy than I am. The Wisdom that created this body bathes it in the Light of Healing rays. I gladly and thankfully step into these rays now and let them course over me, around me, and through me, and I emerge clean and fresh and hale and hearty and enthusiastic and whole. I go forth vibrating with health, glowing with health, at-one with health. I am health, and I thank the Great Healer for this truth.

It is so because I let it be so and nothing short of perfect health is mine today.

You Are Now Ready to Be Infused with Vitalizing Health-Energy

As always throughout this book, your *Psycho-Image Materialization Affirmation* prepares your subconscious mind for the influx of whatever it is you need—in this case, health. Practice the above *Affirmation* until you can *feel* the truth of the statement: *I am health!* You may have to repeat it several times, but it's well worth this minor effort, don't you think? After all, the Divine Healer with Cosmic Accuracy does all the rest!

Bill D., of Bronx, New York, had to mentalize the *Affirmation* dozens of times before it went to work, simply because his mind was so very much cluttered with superfluous thoughts, ideas, and beliefs. But when it worked—*it worked!* And it will work for you once you become at-one with the Divine Healer.

Once the soil of your subconscious mind is cultivated by *Psycho-Image Materialization Affirmation #3*, you are ready to let *New Miracle Dynamics Mind Activator #3* trigger your dormant, latent, but vitalizing Health-energy. Here is the secret key to making the Great Physician work for you.

New Miracle Dynamics Mind Activator #3

"The first wealth," said Emerson, "is health."

Yes, health is *your* first wealth, your riches, your fortune. What is all the money in the world if you are too ill to enjoy it? Health is wealth.

You do *not* want to be like the beggar who failed to realize that he was sitting on wealth all the time that he was begging for a living. You do *not* want to be one of those people who fail to realize that Health is a Divine Gift, that *you are health!* The Health you need, desire, want, is at your disposal right here and now!

"Truth is victory," to find truth is to conquer. The joy of the Infinite is ever with us, but we do not know this truth. We are like the begger in the story who had been begging all his life in the same place. He wanted to be rich, but he was poor. When he died they found a treasure of gold buried just under the place where he had been begging. If he had only known how easy it was to be rich! True knowledge of the Self does not lead to salvation: it is salvation.

Bhagavad Gita

Okay—now you know the Truth—act upon it!

"If he had only known . . ." Yes, indeed, if we had only knowh that the wealth of health we need is right here at our fingertips! Now you know! Act upon it! Prepare your subconscious mind with *Psycho-Image Materialization Affirmation #3*. Then make contact with the Divine Healer with *New Miracle Dynamics Mind Activator #3*. Then—Psycho-Image it!

Psycho-Image what?

By following the preceding technique, thousands of people just like you have healed themselves of ailments such as migraine headaches, arthritis, lumbago, rheumatism, and even lameness. You can do the same.

Bad leg? *Psycho-Image* it as whole!

Soreness? Weakness? Lethargy? Bronchitis, colds, fevers—*Psycho-Image* it as over and done with!

See yourself dancing, frolicking through green fields, romping in the sun. Shut out false appearances to the contrary and *Psycho-Image* yourself as healthy, happy, and whole!

How to Use Psycho-Image Materialization the Way Sandra L. Did to Heal Herself

Sandra L. Lives in Wichita, Kansas, and is but one of countless individuals who have had their health restored through contacting superhuman healing powers with the use of dynamic *Psycho-Image Materialization* exercises. I received this letter from Sandra recently.

Dear Mr. Laurence:

I must tell you right off that I am suffering acute and severe pain. I have crippling arthritis. The fingers of both my hands are swollen and practically useless. My legs are no better. Even though I'm only 41, I have to walk as if I were a crippled old woman. I could tell you stories of years of excruciating pain and suffering. I've had this horrible disease for six years and relief seems impossible. A friend told me about your knowledge of psychic and spiritual matters and, in desperation, I am writing to you to ask: Is there a supernatural way to cure arthritis?"

Sandra went on to explain to me why she was writing at all:

"I'm scared to death, Mr. Laurence," she confessed. "I saw Walter Cronkite on the CBS news the other night and he said the government was now checking into the possible connection of such products as Excedrin P.M. and cancer! My God, Mr. Laurence, I've been eating pills like these for years! I don't want to get cancer—that would be worse than my arthritis! What can I do? Please help me before I go completely crazy with worry."

It so happens that I, too, saw the broadcast to which Sandra referred. Here we have just another instance of possible cancer-causing agents in some of our most familiar products! It seems we are living in an age when we can no longer trust even the finest of medicines! No wonder Sandra wanted to try extra-human means to health. Many people are turning to Divine aid in these times of uncertainty, and I don't blame them. Centuries of mysticism prove that metaphysical healing practices *do* work!

I responded to Sandra's cry for help as soon as I could. I mailed her the *Psycho-Image Materialization Affirmation #3* and the *New Miracle Dynamics Mind Activator #3*. Just two weeks later I received this remarkable letter:

Dear, *dear* Mr. Laurence:

It's a miracle! It has to be! Oh, I'm so excited I can hardly write. And *I'm* doing the writing! My first letter to you was written for me by a friend—I couldn't move my fingers or hold a pen! Now I can! Easily! It's simply amazing.

You just won't believe what happened to me. I must tell you. I took the material you sent me—the *Psycho-Image* techniques—and got alone with them and started practicing them right away. I began one night, just before going to sleep. You got me to thinking about God, about Divine Agency, about the Great Physician and the Superhuman Healer. And that night I dreamed of Him! Yes, I dreamed of this great white Being, sort of an Angel, and He told me in my dream that new life and health was coursing through my whole system. When I awoke the next morning I felt a strange, but beautiful feeling of complete release, of peace, of relaxation. I can hardly describe this feeling.

When I went to fix my breakfast I was astounded to discover that I could use my fingers almost effortlessly. I ate like a horse for the first time in a long time. I was so excited, I ran to the telephone to tell the miraculous news to my friend. Without thinking, I dialed the phone. Maybe you don't know what it means for an arthritic to dial a phone, but it's a blessing!

After the call I ran into my bedroom and resumed practicing *New Miracle Dynamics* the way you told me to. I lay down and Psycho-Imaged myself laughing and running through beautiful, sunlit fields, playing like a little girl. Then I pictured myself playing a piano (something I had to give up when arthritis struck me down). It was while I was in this happy frame of mind when the most uncanny thing happened. My dream image Angel appeared in my mind and spoke to me. I won't repeat what He told me (that has to remain my secret), but as He talked, it was as if white light was spilling all over my body, covering me from head to foot.

All I can say is I must have fallen asleep. When I opened my eyes and looked around I saw by the clock that three hours had passed! If that wasn't shock enough, a greater shock occurred immediately. I *leapt* out of bed! My legs moved easily, freely!

To make a long but wonderful story short: I called my doctors and arranged to see them the next morning. When I bounced into their office, they couldn't believe their eyes. I was youthful, buoyant, energetic, arthritis-free! I was completely healed of my painful disease! In just two days that crippling condition was absolutely, totally gone!

My doctors were delighted that I was whole, but they still won't believe me when I tell them how this miracle happened. They insist on believing that I went to other doctors and got treated. That's okay with me. I don't care now whether they believe me or not. I'm deliriously happy, and that's all that counts. At least I know about *Psycho-Image Materialization* and its wonder-working power in my life. All I had to do was follow your instructions and lie back and receive the perfect health I've longed for.

I sure don't take pills any more. Those days are gone forever—along with the pain! I'm jogging every morning now. Tomorrow I'm going hiking with some of the ladies from the neighborhood. I feel so alive!

Mystic Secret of Psycho-Image Materialization Brings Instant Health and Healing to You and Your Loved Ones

The Great Healer from the invisible, subconscious side of life will come to your aid, no matter what your problem, when you follow these instructions:

1. Form in your mind a clear Psycho-Image of yourself or an ailing loved one, but picture this person as completely whole and healthy—even if they appear to be diseased, crippled, sick, or unhealthy. Always picture the person in your mind as totally well.

2. Select a place where you can practice your *Psycho-Image Materialization* exercises without disturbance. Either lie down or sit comfortably in a relaxing chair.

3. Close your eyes and take a few deep breaths, slowly inhaling, slowly exhaling. Be aware of your whole body relaxing, from head to toe.

4. In your mind's eye form your own Psycho-Image of the patient (yourself or someone else) completely whole and amazingly healthy. If, for instance, you or a loved one is afficted with a tumor or rheumatism or migraine headaches or anemia (or any other disease), Psycho-Image the person as free of any and all disease. Do *not* picture the patient as he or she *appears* to be (ill) but as God meant him or her to be (well).

5. You are now prepared to recite the power words of *Psycho-Image Materialization Affirmation #3* and *New Miracle Dynamics Mind Activator #3*. Read, say aloud, or mentalize each of these.

6. Permit yourself to feel the elation and happiness that comes with full and complete recovery. Express your gratitude for this Divine Healing *prior to receipt*, as Jesus did.

    Say aloud:

    "Thank you, Father, for this miraculous healing."

    If you are Psycho-Imaging for someone else, state:

    This Psycho-Image exercise is for _____.

    Then say:

    Thank you, Father, for this miraculous healing.

    You can express this early gratitude for the simple

     but beautiful reason that the Great Physician is already operating upon you (or the loved one) even as you are Psycho-Imaging.

7. Do not by any means permit images of disease, ill health, or pain and suffering to enter your mind. Always Psycho-Image perfect health.

8. Take a break. Relax. Give yourself a few moments to absorb the startling truth that higher-than-human agencies are working for you even as you sit or lie peaceably and relaxed.

9. Repeat the *Psycho-Image Materialization Affirmation* and *New Miracle Dynamics Mind Activator*. After three exercises, pause.

10. End the session and proceed with your daily life, knowing beyond a doubt that the Great Physician is healing you (or the loved one).

The Mystic Secret of Healing Now Revealed to You

When Christ said to the crippled man, "Get up and walk," *he undoubtedly saw a perfectly whole man*! If Divine Healing occurs in the mind, and if Christ imaged an unhealthy man instead of a whole one, no healing would have taken place, according to the law of cause and effect. You do not Psycho-Image a sick person; you deal only with Divine Ideas of man, a spiritual being; otherwise, you may take on the vibrations of pain. From what we know about *Psycho-Image Materialization*, Christ must have imaged only a perfectly whole man. Of course, He probably saw the false appearance of disease, but He did not permit his subconscious mind to hold a picture of that condition.

Healing is not *creating* a healthy, whole physical body; it is Psycho-Imaging the truth that perfection of body already exists, spiritually speaking. You must recognize the fact that a Spiritual Body imbues the physical body. It is not required of you to Psycho-Image this Spiritual Body, but you should be aware of It as a Divine Idea, that the power and love of the

Cosmos flows through it freely, uninhibited, undiseased, perfect.

Recognize the difference between fact and truth. It is a fact that disease exists; it is not a truth that it *must* exist. *Ill health is a physical experience but not a spiritual reality.* Disease, therefore, is a fact but not a truth. You do not tell a person in pain that there is no pain. Of course, there is. But you recognize pain and suffering as *unnecessary*. It was a *fact* that human beings do not leave this planet, but it was not a *truth*. To remain earthbound is not a necessity. If our forefathers had learned how to leave this globe, they would have initiated space travel. So always remember: Behind the appearance of disease, *Perfect health is*.

How to Use Psycho-Image Materialization Across Great Distances for the Healing of Others

Edna P., of Albany, New York, Psycho-Imaged her sister as perfectly whole and cured her in fifteen minutes! Her sister lives in Sarramento, California.

Jim L., of Orlando, Florida, cured his mother of heart ailments with *Psycho-Image Materialization* exercises, and she was residing 2000 miles away.

Philip M. healed his wife of a tumor. He lived in Toronto, Canada; his wife was hospitalized in Houston, Texas.

This should prove something important to you. Neither time nor space can interfere with Divine Agency. The Great Physician operates in a timeless and spaceless dimension—for you.

Healing takes place to the degree that you implant the proper images in your subconscious mind. By practicing *Psycho-Image Materialization Affirmation #3* and *New Miracle Dynamics Mind Activator #3*, you seed or sow your own subconscious mind, and Universal Mind reproduces your Psycho-Images in the physical body—no matter where that body may be! Remain cognizant of the fact that you are using a Supernatural Power, calling upon It to aid you, succor you, help you, heal you (or a loved one). As you produce potent

Psycho-Images in your own mind, which is actually an integral part of Divine Mind, you reach the mind of your patient—even across great distances! You can erase pain and suffering in others when you first Psycho-Image peace and perfection in your own subconscious mind. The Great Physician does the rest!

You are, then, entering into a partnership with Supernatural Forces: you Psycho-Image perfection and It heals!

How Evelyn T. Used the "Healing Oil" Psycho-Image to Cure Her Chronic Arthritis

Evelyn T. of Nashville, Tennessee was confined to a wheelchair for three years, a woman severely crippled by arthritis. Her legs, arms, and spine were all affected by this terrible disease. Therefore, she was unable to enjoy her own children, who needed her love and attention. In short, her whole life was one long misery. Pills, treatments, lotions, ointments—nothing seemed to help this poor woman.

In discussing the Psycho-Image power that would heal Evelyn's body completely, an interesting thing came out. Evelyn's husband had deserted her and the children a few years before. Since then she had been harboring tremendous resentment against him. This is natural enough, to be sure, but negative emotions are body-killers! I had to educate Evelyn in this regard before we could get on with the healing.

It is wise to remember that negative thoughts, feelings, and emotions undermine your health. And it is wise to "clear the mind" of these destructive agencies before using healing Psycho-Images. Otherwise the Psycho-Images can be shortcircuited by the negativity! In my research into the power of Mind over physical suffering, I learned much about the insidious destruction caused by hidden negative emotions, particularly in regard to arthritis. As Edgar White Burrill points out in his article "The True Healer"[1]: "Do you know the medical profession has found that arthritis is the result of

---

[1]Edgar White Burrill, "The True Healer," *Science of Mind*, August, 1978.

chronic resentment? . . . Look back over the past years and
see if you haven't had something bothering you."

This is what I had Evelyn do, and to "clear" away her
negativity, she used the following Psycho-Image Prayer:

> *O healing Physician of the Universe, cleanse my
> every thought, my every pore, my every heartbeat!
> Wash me clean and make me whole, healthy, and
> supremely happy!*

Thus able to rid herself of her husband's negative mem-
ory, Evelyn could successfully employ the "Healing Oil"
Psycho-Image to cure her crippling disease. She was out of
her wheelchair and running and playing with her children in
four days! Complete healing was hers. It astounded skeptical
doctors and cynical neighbors. Evelyn says nothing to anyone
about the magical cure. She continues to take the doctors'
advice, she takes pills when pain strikes, but the healing itself, total and complete, is fast moving her toward complete
freedom from medicine.

Your Miracle Method for Curing Arthritis

Whether you have arthritis or not, the following
Psycho-Image power will help you. Whatever your malady,
or even if you use the following to heal someone else, it will
work miracles in your life. Read the steps carefully a few
times. "Clear" the air with the above prayer, and then do the
following exercise:

1. Get alone with yourself. Lie down or sit comfortably
   in a chair with your head supported.
2. Close your eyes and Psycho-Image a huge crystal
   bottle of oil tipping to anoint your whole body.
3. Completely relax and permit this magic oil to soak
   you through and through, not only on the surface of
   your body, but *feel* it permeating your every muscle
   and joint. Follow the flowing, healing oil with your
   mind through your whole body. Guide it mentally to

the areas afflicted with pain—and *feel* its soothing power. Repeat this part three times.

4. Say the following Psycho-Image Formula to yourself:

> *I let go and let Higher Physicians heal me completely. I bathe now in the healing oil of the Universe, letting it permeate all areas of my body that are crippled with arthritis (or whatever ailment bothers you). Through the love of Supernatural Healers my damaged being is now restored to perfect health.*

5. Envision yourself in Psycho-Images keeping an appointment with Divine Doctors. Psycho-Image yourself in the office (if this treatment is for a loved one, picture that person in the doctor's office). Now hear the Great White Physician saying to you: "I am delighted to report that tests have come back and show that you are completely free of arthritis. This is an amazing breakthrough for metaphysical healing, and I am so happy that it has happened to you!"

6. You say mentally:

> *I thank you with all my heart, doctor. Thank you, thank you, THANK YOU!*

(This is your equivalent to *gratitude prior to receipt* in that you are being thankful before your arthritis (or whatever) disappears.)

7. Repeat the following Psycho-Image Formula to yourself:

> *Through the agency of Superior Physicians healing oils infuse, permeate, and heal every area in my body afflicted with* _____ (insert name of disease).

8. End the session and go about your daily business with a *grateful* heart.

How a Woman Lost 88 Pounds Through the Secret of Psycho-Image Materialization

I first heard from Anita M. of Scranton, Pennsylvania after she'd read one of my Parker books, *The Miracle Power of Believing*.[2] In her welcomed letter she wrote: "I have a terrible problem, Mr. Laurence. I'm so overweight I look like a blimp! Please help me. Tell me what I can do to lose some weight. I weigh 198 pounds. That's about 90 pounds too much! Please help me."

The weight-releasing method I gave Anita will help anyone with a similar problem. By following this easy-to-use program Anita lost 88 pounds in less than three months! The loss of unsightly weight opened new doors of fun and happiness for her. It will do the same for you!

The New Miracle Dynamics Program for Losing Weight Fast

Follow the easy steps of this program at least once a day.

1. Say this mantra:

   Agni-Mars, god of fire, Burn away all excess weight from my body.

2. Psycho-Image a great fire *melting* away excess weight within your system. Direct this fire to any area of your body with your mind.

3. Fire has two major properties, not one: flame and heat. After "seeing" the divine fire melt your excess weight, visualize the *heat* evaporating the melted weight.

4. Repeat steps 1 to 3 with your eyes closed and in a relaxed position. Permit yourself to feel your excess weight melting and evaporating away from you.

---

[2]Theodor Laurence, *The Miracle Power of Believing*, West Nyack, New York: Parker Publishing Company, Inc.

5. Go about your daily business with *gratitude*.

How Supernatural Healing Aids Modern Medicine and You

If you are under any medication or doctor's aid, by all means continue their use. Supernatural healing forces should be used in conjunction with modern medicine, not instead of it. If you are under a doctor's care, he, too, will be amazed and pleased at your so-called impossible recovery and health!

You are a most potent channel of Cosmic Forces. With the knowledge and help of superphysical agencies at your disposal, no illness, disease, or injury can long undermine your health and happiness. With the help of this book you are now in a position to call upon the same sources of healing as did Edgar Cayce. Use Psycho-Image Materialization wisely for yourself and for others.

Your New Miracle Dynamics Key to Super Health

Even the most strongly resistant disease and the so-called "incurables" can be cured with Psycho-Image Materialization. The following failproof technique is designed to help you overcome any illness, as it has helped thousands before you.

1. Choose a place in your home where you can be quietly alone. Sit in a comfortable chair or lie down peacefully. Psycho-Image relaxation as a fluid. See this fluid pouring all over you like honey, permeating your every pore, your every cell and muscle. Feel it relaxing you totally.

2. Close your eyes, and for a few moments just watch this warm, relaxing fluid bathe you—particularly in those areas you intend to heal.

3. Repeat the following Psycho-Image Mind Activator to yourself mentally:

Through the power of unseen forces I stand
in the healing rays of super color-rays, absorb-
ing all the healthful vibrations. I know with
sureness and confidence that no illness can de-
feat me, and I am eternally grateful NOW for
this truth. I permit supernatural forces to heal
me through and through.

4. Psycho-Image these supernatural forces as Great Physicians. In your mind's eye see them attending to you, repairing damages, healing illness. Feel yourself responding completely and positively to this Great Healing.

5. Repeat the following *New Miracle Dynamics Mind Activator* daily:

Even though my physical body goes about its
daily business in a normal way, supernatural
forces are healing me in a supernormal way.
For this I am most grateful.

Put Yourself in This List of Miraculously Healed People

John D., of Dallas, Texas, suffered a terrible accident on his job. A piece of flying metal pierced his right eye. Most people agreed that it would take a miracle to heal John. And that miracle occurred when his wife Ellen used the above technique *for* him! Full sight and complete healing was restored to John's eye in two weeks!

Through the use of the above healing technique, Sandra R., of Roanoke, Virginia, escaped breast surgery. Just prior to her appointment with doctors for final examinations, Sandra—who feared and hated the idea of breast surgery—began using the technique as outlined for her. When she went for examination, the physicians were amazed to discover that Sandra's tumor had completely dissolved. Surgery was now out of the question. She simply didn't need it!

Ken F., of Spokane, Washington, wrote:

My doctor is furious with me! I was having terrible sinus attacks until I started using Psycho-Image Materialization techniques for curing myself. I went to show my doctor the miracle of supernatural healing, and in the office were four other people with severe sinus conditions. I told them about Psycho-Image Materialization—and every one of them was cured! My doctor is goodheartedly furious because supernatural healing is undermining his business!"

Supernatural Healing Is Really Natural— if It Isn't Happening in Your Life, Something's Wrong

When you are in tune with Higher Powers, you know intuitively that the so-called supernatural is really natural— TO YOU! To others, it looks like strange and uncanny miracles are occurring!

You have the power to contact the mystic secrets of Supernatural Forces. You do this through the applied use of Psycho-Image Materialization techniques and programs.

Start now to abolish all disease, illness, and pain from yourself and your loved ones. Time and space have no meaning here. You can use Psycho-Image Materialization secrets to cure others who are many miles away.

Remember this: the unlimited healing power of Supernatural Beings is at your beck and call every hour of every day. You needn't suffer any more. You are just a Psycho-Image away from Divine Healing. Get in touch with it through the techniques in this chapter.

4

Magnetize Unexpected Windfalls, Surprising Good Fortune, And Phenomenal Luck

There is a psychospiritual vibration of prosperity that you can tap into and channel through your own personal life—if you know the mystic secret. That secret is *Psycho-Image Materialization*, the means by which you will contact and *command* higher forces that will automatically respond to your every need, wish or desire. Amazing? You bet it is! And you will be amazed as it works for you!

In ancient times, when men and women tuned in to this remarkable vibration of prosperity, they were called mystics. The mystics were the first to disclose the secret of attracting good to oneself via metaphysical means. Accordingly, the mystics taught methods and techniques that were diametrically opposed to wordly teachings (much as Jesus did). They called this vibration of prosperity the Way. Whenever they tuned in to this Way, amazing and satisfying events occurred in their lives, setting them apart from the average run of people, for they consequently enjoyed great prosperity, peace, and happiness. You will do likewise!

The mystic spent months, sometimes years, in a cave; you need only spend five to fifteen minutes in the privacy of your home!

The mystic engaged in strict regimens of self-discipline; you need do nothing but desire fervently!

The mystic used long and complicated spells, prayers, and chants; you simply use ready-made *Psycho-Image Materialization Affirmations* and *New Miracle Dynamics Mind Activators*!

Such is the astounding progress of mysticism. In fact, when you use *Psycho-Image Materialization* techniques, you are indeed a "New Mystic." And, like the mystics of old, you will tap in to that invisible Source of plenty and abundance, you will channel that vibration of prosperity, and you will follow the Way.

The time has come for you to reap a harvest of riches. So, get ready to be enriched beyond your wildest dreams when superhuman forces respond to your needs! You have worked and slaved long enough—you deserve the uplifting gifts you are about to receive. Yes, it is time for you to receive all you have earned through faith and hard labor, and you shall— from this universe's mightiest power, the Great Materializer. All you have to do is contact this Source, let It know you are ready and willing to receive Its aid, be grateful *now*—and leave the rest to It!

Just follow these simple instructions:

1. Get alone with yourself in a quiet, comfortable place.
2. Close your eyes, take a few deep breaths, banish all obstructing thoughts from your mind.
3. Read (aloud or mentally) the following *Psycho-Image Materialization Affirmation.*

As you slowly read this *Affirmation* (read it twice), your mind will become attuned to paranormal frequencies of vibration. It will raise *your* mental vibrations to that level of reality that ancient mystics contacted for fast and miraculous help.

Psycho-Image Materialization Affirmation #4

I am surrounded by and immersed in the Pure and Living Spirit of God, the Fount of Limitless Abundance. My Word is the Word of God, and its utterance is Law. Everything I undertake to do is positive, creative, and prosperous. My every thought, word, and deed is inspired and guided by Divine Order and right action. I know that whatever I do, wherever I do it, is directed by God, my guiding Father.

Right action directs my every move, internally and externally. My mind is alive with the consciousness of right action, which creates unending prosperity. I am surrounded by and im-

mersed in eternal Abundance, which is always taking concrete and material form in my life according to the molds I give It to fill.

As the Spirit of God flows through me to all around me, so it is with money, success, and prosperity. Whatever I touch turns to gold, opulence, and happiness. My fullness, my joy, my wealth, my success, and my happiness—all are made manifest by the inexorable flow of Abundance towards me.

I have a deep and abiding understanding of the unique position I occupy in the Universe. I am uniquely individual as each and every one of us is uniquely individual. We are all One, and yet the Divine incarnates in me in a special way that individualizes me. Therefore, I have no desire to compare myself with another or to envy another's prosperity, for I have my very own Abundance with which to express the fullness and happiness of life. Right now my personal experience reflects all good, and prosperity manifests in my individual life. As above, so below. United with all selves, I am yet myself, full and complete, individual and unique, and I need compete with no one for the prosperity that is already mine.

As my success and happiness is continuous and eternal, so is my gratitude and thankfulness. In this state of appreciation, I behold the wondrous workings of the Living Spirit. There is a Divine magnet in me to which all people are attracted, and everyone I meet loves this inner self of mine and appreciates its value. Everyone I meet is drawn to me, directed to me, guided to me for Divine purposes of mutual benefit. An irresistible gravity attracts into my purview all those to whose prosperity I can contribute and those who will contribute to my prosperity. I need not coerce or will. I know that the Divine Director is orchestrating this symphony of pros-

> *perity for my sake. This Truth liberates me from all thoughts of lack and limitation. I know that money, success, and prosperity are effects of the great Cause which is God, my Father. The spiritual idea of money and prosperity is in my mind right now. Abundance is mine, and I accept it, with deep gratitude.*
>
> *I am prosperous because I am prosperity incarnate.*
>
> *And so it is.*

Invisible, Beneficent Forces Are Now Activating in Your Life

You have just triggered supernormal powers through the power of your own thought! Expect miracles! Anticipate wonders! Prepare yourself for the receipt of riches of all kinds, for you have attuned your mind to the vibration of prosperity.

As the *Affirmation* implies, you do not have to work and slave, will and coerce, in order to receive those wonderful riches that are yours by right. Like the magicians of old, you—the New Magician—will sit back and permit abundance to flow freely into your life. You will utilize the Magical Formula for Accruing Riches Instantly! How? By contacting Infinite Powers.

Here's the mystic secret.

New Miracle Dynamics Mind Activator #4

No magician or mystic ever labored as common men labored. Mystics, saints, seers, and magicians were often looked upon with awe. Food, money, travel, clothing, houses, supernatural powers—all came to them via seemingly magical means. They were able to tune in to invisible sources of supply—just as you are now doing! Common folk rarely understood the magician, even when he endeavored to explain the means by which he received wealth, supply, and abundance. The magician tried to explain that he was in tune with supernatural forces— something few ordinary people can comprehend. But your *Affirmation* fertilizes your subconscious mind and prepares you to understand and to *use* the mystic secret to riches overflowing.

Use These Ten-Steps for Accruing Fast Riches Through Psycho-Image Materialization

1. Invoke supernatural aid every day by using the attuning *Affirmation*. Close your eyes and go into the quiet place within, that magical place that bypasses the natural and makes instant contact with the supernatural.

   Repeat the *Affirmation* until all outside fears, doubts, and worries are silenced in you. As you transcend these obstacles, harmony and tranquility will be yours. Contact with higher forces of Mind automatically follows.

2. At least once a day sit quietly and Psycho-Image yourself in dramas and scenes in which you are always receiving amazing windfalls, phenomenal good luck, and unexpected good fortune—in love, money, opportunities, contests, games. Make a list of the wonderful things you wish to see happen to you.

   If you like entering contests, see yourself receiving mail or phone calls informing you that you are the supreme winner. See yourself receiving a beautiful new car, a fantastic dream house, furs, jewels, and cash, cash, CASH!

   If you are in business, visualize yourself receiving

remarkable assets, increased income, phenomenal sales, etc.

If you are a housewife, see yourself receiving unexpected windfalls. Why not a thousand-dollar bill on the sidewalk? Perhaps news that you have been chosen the winner of cash prizes, trips abroad, new clothes, etc.

3. Every day, immediately after reciting the attuning *Affirmation*, make yourself a magnet for riches, money, and abundance in all things. Psycho-Image yourself as a powerful magnet, irresistible, drawing all kinds of good fortune to yourself. *Feel* riches, goods and fun coming toward you at prodigious speed!

4. Before saying the *Affirmation*, make a list of ten things you want desperately and would like supernatural helpers to provide for you. Barbara L.'s list looks like this.

I desperately need the following items:

1. A great job with a fantastic salary.
2. An unexpected windfall of $10,000.
3. The "perfect man" to come into my life.
4. Popularity, magnetism, and attractiveness.
5. A Caribbean cruise.
6. Love and marriage and a happy relationship.
7. So much money that I'll never have to worry again.
8. Friends and acquaintances who will do everything in their power to make me happier, healthier, and richer.
9. A brand new super car.
10. The winning of every contest and game I enter.

5. Recite mentally or orally the *Affirmation* three times, then do this: Remember that each day of the

week is named after a supernatural god. Each day
say these magic formulas:

MONDAY: *O Moon Goddess, fill my life with the silver of your power in the form of money.*

TUESDAY: *O Zeus, God of Might, rain thy beneficence upon me this day.*

WEDNESDAY: *O Mercury, God of Rapid Flight, quickly bring to me great riches and wealth.*

THURSDAY: *O Thor, God of Thunder, send thy bolts of power to blast away all obstacles to my enrichment.*

FRIDAY: *O Venus, Goddess of Beauty, make my whole life one of rich, luxurious beauty.*

SATURDAY: *O Saturn, mighty God of Regularity, I invoke your power for regular and steady flow of income.*

SUNDAY: *O mighty Sun, shine your golden rays down upon me in the form of real gold, money, riches, rewards, winnings.*

6. Insight is power. Each day make it a habit to Psycho-Image yourself receiving profound insights into money-making, wealth-accumulation, and contest-winning. When a thought or idea emerges in your mind during your use of this magical formula, *act on it!* Sometimes a mere number comes to mind. It is often a winning number!

7. Each day Psycho-Image yourself receiving divine help from on high. Receive super positive thoughts,

ideas and directions to make your life richer and happier. Open yourself through the *Affirmation* to gifts of peace, goodness, love, and, especially—MONEY!

8. Infuse yourself with wealth-magnetizing power saying three times each day: "Great wealth is my birthright. I now claim this wealth and permit it to enter my life through supernatural means."

9. Use the *Affirmation* every day to attune your mind to Divine Mind, to supernatural agencies that want to help you toward a richer, fuller life. By daily use you are programming yourself into receiving amazing unexpected money and wealth. As often as you can, chant:

I permit myself to receive;
In God I do believe;
Though Fate tosses and pitches,
I receive lasting riches.

10. Program your higher mind with the AFFIRMATION to stay in direct contact with higher-than-human forces of the universe, forces that will come to your aid in your time of need. There is nothing to be denied you when you are at-one with universal powers flowing through your mind into concrete and exciting materialization!

New Miracle Dynamics Makes Ancient Truths Work for You in Modern Ways

The preceding Mind Activator is an Eastern way of saying: "Let go and let God." Simply by reading it over and over, you are adjusting the vibrations of your own mentality to super-natural vibrations of abundance and plenty. Once you have done so, start over. Do this:

1. Get alone with yourself.
2. Recite orally or mentally the *Psycho-Image Affirmation*.

3. Recite orally or mentally the *Mind Activator*.
4. Begin visualizing your heart's desires. Envision what
    you want, see it clearly in your mind's eye, infuse it
    with feeling, expectation, and need. Psycho-Image
    your wishes, dreams, and desires—and watch them
    materialize in your life right before your eyes!

These are the very steps that many others like you have
followed in order to make ancient mystic secrets manifest in
their modern lives.

Joanna R., of Tulsa, Oklahoma, simply wanted a man
who would love and cherish her. She practiced the preceding
Psycho-Image technique, and no sooner had she completed
mentalizing the *Psycho-Image Mind Activator*, then a knock
came to her door. There stood a tall handsome stranger who
told her a remarkable story of how he had been passing by,
felt an irresistible urge to knock on her door, and couldn't
defy it! Joanna and Robert are now happily married, and
Robert says: "I can't explain it to this day. I was on my way to
a business meeting, hurrying, I might add. But it was like I'd
run into an invisible barrier right there on the sidewalk. Then
a part of my mind I'd never felt before seemed to open. I
suddenly felt uplifted, excited, enthused—for no reason at all!
I looked at this house and before I knew what I was doing, I
was knocking on the door. This lovely woman opened it and
her eyes mesmerized me. I was tongue-tied, but I knew what
I was feeling; something I thought I'd never feel again: Love.
And I somehow sensed that Joanna was feeling the same
thing—this perfect stranger was in love with me! I've always
thought of love as an emotion, not a force, but believe me, on
that day it was a definite, undeniable, magnetic Force!"

Today, Joanna delights to exclaim: "It was miraculous! In
just minutes, I went from devastating loneliness to excruciating happiness! Robert is all I ever dreamed of in a man!"

Sam D., a door-to-door salesman in Canton, Ohio, practiced *Psycho-Image Materialization* for only one day. The
following day, walking the pavement in search of a sale, he
approached a house to sell his wares. He never made it to the
door. When he entered the yard and closed the gate behind

him, a huge, ferocious dog attacked him! Frightened out of his
wits, Sam turned to escape the yard. The dog blocked his
exit. Sam turned to run across the lawn. The dog bounded in
front of him, stopping him dead. Sam whirled in horror, heart
pounding, sweat dripping from his forehead, and tried to run
in the opposite direction. The dog, snarling, baring his teeth,
leapt in front of him again and stopped him. Sam's only out
was to run around the house. The dog seemed to permit this.
Sam ran for his life around the house, through the backyard,
and climbed over a fence. The dog gave chase, scaled the
fence in one mighty leap, and took after Sam again, hot on his
heels.

Sam, now breathless and fearing a heart attack from the
severe tension of this frightful event, ran as fast as his legs
could carry him. He was looking over his shoulder constantly,
seeing the fangs of that dog close on his heels. Suddenly, Sam
fell, tripping over a fallen tree in a grassy lot. He rolled over
onto his back to protect himself from the charging beast, but
to his utter surprise, the dog simply stopped and sat down!
The dog's eyes now looked benign and friendly. His tail was
wagging. His fangs were concealed. He cocked his head and
peered at Sam. Sam, getting his breath back, afraid to move,
felt something hard beneath him, causing him pain. He
shifted his position and looked down. There he saw, sticking
from the earth, a rusty metal bar, attached to something.
Suddenly the dog came up to the spot, sniffed at it repeatedly,
and kept whining at Sam, as if to tell him something. Sam got
the "message," and unearthed the thing he had been sitting
on. The metal turned out to be a handle. It was attached to a
metal box, so old and weathered that when Sam lifted it out,
it crumbled to rusty dust. And there before his eyes was a
cache of jewels! Those jewels were later appraised at a value
of $150,000! Sam says:

> "What really amazed me was that just as I was
> approaching that house I was Psycho-Imaging the
> woman buying $50 worth of my products. I thought
> $50 was an immense sum of money for me to make
> in one day! But that dog! I believe now that super-

natural forces made that animal guide me to the spot where the jewelry was stored. I was in tune with paranormal forces and I couldn't help but become rich. What a windfall! It enabled me to quit my job and take a vacation in Hawaii and then open my own business! And I didn't have to do anything except Psycho-Image myself receiving money! Mystic forces did all the work for me!"

Psycho-Image Materialization created instant good fortune in the life of Edna L., of Seattle, Washington, in February recently. And all she had to do was Psycho-Image what she wanted! Edna explains:

"I did the *Psycho-Image Materialization Affirmation* and the *New Miracle Dynamics Mind Activator* only three times—all in one day. I was so eager to get it working in my life that I did them once in the morning, then at noon, and again that evening, in bed. I got results the very next morning! You see, I awoke feeling depressed. I mean, I just didn't feel like going to work. I'm a maid in a local motel. I lay there in bed, and a picture jumped into my mind, a picture of the women I work with, all of them old and tired and worn out. And I said to myself: 'Is this how I'm going to look a few years from now?' My next thought flogged me: how was I to live if I didn't go to work? This thought was followed by another.

"I suddenly recalled that one of my co-workers had asked me about the Ouija board. Another had once wanted to know about reading auras. I had been studying these things, but I hadn't had time to answer the questions: I was so overworked! But on this particular morning my subconscious mind filled me with an idea: *sell my knowledge*! I immediately called in sick and talked to those two women who had asked me questions. I don't even know why I said this, but I told them I was starting my own business and that for a fee I would reveal some occult secrets to them. They were delighted, and that night they came over and paid me to tell them.

"That began my business. I placed ads in newspapers advertising my services. Within a week I had received over $500 in the mail! I couldn't believe my good fortune! Why, just a week before I was making minimum wage and my bank account was overdrawn! Now here I am raking in at least $500 a week. If this keeps up—and I'm confident that it will!—I'll be making $2000 a month or $24,000 each year! God, I'm so happy!"

Philip Y., of Gardena, California, used *Psycho-Image Materialization* in a most unorthodox fashion. He Psycho-Imaged himself winning horse races! He says:

"I'm not really a gambling man but when I read about PSYCHO-IMAGE MATERIALIZATION I thought to myself, why not let supernatural forces materialize winning race horses for me? So, here's what I did: I took typed copies of the *Psycho-Image Materialization Affirmation #4* and *New Miracle Dynamics Mind Activator #4* to the racetrack with me. I hadn't been to a track in years, but it felt right somehow. I simply moved through the crowds reading my secret material, preparing my subconscious mind for supernatural aid. Then I took a race form and closed my eyes and let my finger be guided to the winning horse. I bought only combination tickets at $6.00 each, which means I'd win something whether the horse came in first, second or third— win, place, or show. Well, the first race I won $18.60, over three times my investment. No fortune, I know, but I was testing *Psycho-Image Materialization*. The second race I bet $18 and won $45.50. The third race I bet $40 and got back over $100! By then I knew it was working— miraculously, inexorably—so I purchased 16 $6 tickets for the next race—and to my astonishment, I won $843! I kept betting this way, increasing my bets with the racetrack's money (I had arrived with only $10 in my wallet!) and winning phenomenal amounts of money in return.

"But the real miracle occurred hours later when I saw the name of the horse in the eighth race: it was *Materializer!* I knew right then that I could not lose. I was walking on air to the window, confident and sure that supernatural forces were indeed guiding me. My mind was definitely in tune with cosmic vibrations. I even felt out of my body, or something like that. I simply bet every dollar I had on that horse: *Materializer.* I watched the race with bated breath. The result was a dead heat—or looked like that until the authorities saw the photos. *Materializer* was proclaimed the winner! In just one day I parlayed $10 into $137,456! And all I had done was Psycho-Image myself winning races!"

The Mystic Secret of Psycho-Imaging Is Yours to Use and Enjoy

You will notice that in the *Psycho-Image Materialization Affirmation #4*, paragraph 2, it states: "I am surrounded by and immersed in eternal Abundance, *which is always taking concrete and material form in my life according to the molds I give It to fill.*"

Do not miss this secret! Just as Joanna, Sam, Edna, and Philip have done, you will do! Learn right now that your personal Psycho-Images—the thoughts you entertain, the way you see yourself, the manner in which you visualize your desires—are *molds!* Absorb this information, digest it, cherish it. You have seen molds into which Jello is poured to give it form. And you've seen cookie molds into which one pours batter to give the cookies form. This principle is the same in your subconscious mind! Your thoughts, feelings, and desires are the batter; your mind is the mold. When you envision yourself (after doing the *Psycho-Image Materialization*

Affirmations and *New Miracle Dynamics Mind Activators)* winning, receiving windfalls, experiencing good fortune, having phenomenal luck, you are in effect making molds, ordering what you want to manifest in your external, physical life. This is *Psycho-Image Materialization* in action! Use it wisely, freely, happily. What do you want? Envision yourself getting it! Prepare your subconscious mind with the Psycho-Image techniques provided for you and then see yourself in your mind's eye receiving all that you want, need, and deserve. And remember: the bigger your mold in the subconscious, the bigger you receive in actual life! So think BIG! Wish BIG! Desire BIG!

Then relax and let Abundance flow into your new and exciting life!

Attract, Command, and Enjoy Love, Respect, Honor, and Fame, The New Miracle Dynamics Way

What would you give for the kind of love that binds fast, that is the principle of existence, that makes others love you, that cannot be bought with labor, that casts out all fear, that is eternal, that is spiritual fire, that conquers all things?

It is precisely this miraculous kind of love that is yours through *Psycho-Image Materialization*. Love is actually a power; not a forceful, hurtful kind of power, but a gentle, everlasting kind of power. But a power, nonetheless! You will possess this power to the degree that you practice the following *Psycho-Image Materialization* exercises, designed to imbue you with the love-power that makes you irresistible to any mate you select! It takes only minutes of your time, for the great Materializer does all the work for you!

This kind of love can bring you respect, honor, and fame. If you are a loving person, you are a giving person. If you are a giving person, you are a generous person. If you are a generous person, you are a sympathetic person. If you are a sympathetic person, you are a helpful person. And, if you are a loving person, you receive respect, honor, and fame.

The question is: how to attract this kind of miracle-working love into *your* life? *New Miracle Dynamics* is the answer. The following exercise will prepare your subconscious mind to receive, channel, and command the kind of love that makes you a magnet for love, respect, honor, and fame.

Psycho-Image Materialization Affirmation #5

Love is God and God is Love, the very fire of the universe, the indwelling flame within each of us, which inspires us, motivates us, animates us, and unites us. Love is the Light which God is, the warming, guiding Light of Life.

God-Love is the eternal fire of creation and I

---

am a spark of that flame, an integral part and expression of the Love that upholds the world. It flows into me, around me, and through me, embracing others as it embraces me. I open myself to Love and It imbues me with Life. It is the center of my being, the central fount from which all other blessings flow. As I yield to Love's influx, I know perfection. As I channel Love, I know percolating joy. As I express Love, I know beauty. As I indwell Love, I love myself and all with whom I come into contact. I and Love are One. I am Love. I accept my life as Love in expression, knowing only peace, serenity, health, strength, and fulfilling companionship. My world is beautified because Love is the center of my world. My attuning of mind, body, and soul to the Divine influx of Love is so complete that nothing but Good goes before me, accompanies me, and follows me. I am made in the image and likeness of Love; I love myself, my life, my world; therefore, I love you, your life, your world.

I accept the Reality of Love's eternity and omnipresence, and I willingly, happily, radiate the Truth of Love. I give thanks daily for this Truth, this Love, this awareness, and I go forth emanating Love in gratitude. Love now flows out of me to whomever I think about, look upon, or touch. All are loved as I am loved.

I know it is so, and so it is!

Why the Secrets of Mysticism Confound the World

All you have to do is get alone with yourself and practice the above *Affirmation* until it works for you. This kind of mystic teaching confounds the world, for the world teaches that you must *work* for love, *demand* love, *earn* love, etc. But you will learn to *command* love, not *de*mand it. Fathers and mothers, wives and husbands who demand love, respect or honor rarely receive it! In fact, they usually attract exactly the opposite! They receive not love, honor, or respect, but ridicule, snickering, and derision, for such people have not yielded to the truth of mystic secrets, the truth that forcefulness is overcome by gentleness, that demands are subdued by requests, that taking is weaker than giving, that resisting is less than yielding.

New Miracle Dynamics Mind Activator #5

Profit right now by the teaching of *Psycho-Image Materialization* that you need do nothing to command love, respect, honor, and fame. You need do nothing but follow the easy instructions in this chapter in order to become a living channel for the Love that conquers all.

Psycho-Image yourself as water. Yes, water! What a common thing! How weak it is, how easily moved, how vagrant! Or is it?

Nothing is weaker than water;
Yet, for attacking what is hard and tough,
Nothing surpasses it, nothing equals it.
The principle, that what is weak overcomes
  what is strong,
And what is yielding conquers what is resistant,
Is known to everyone.
Yet few men utilize it profitably in practice.

Tao Teh King LXXVIII

How Cora L. Found Supreme Happiness Through Psycho-Image Materialization

A woman once wrote to me and asked: "Am I too old to be thinking of marriage?" This woman is 71 years of age. She reminds me of Cora L., a 60-year-old woman in Baltimore, Maryland.

Cora's husband died and, having no children, sisters, brothers, parents, or near relatives, she was desperately lonely. No amount of civic activity or socializing could comfort her. Such activities could not fill that deep and dark void lonely people suffer.

Crushed by the barren life she was leading, Cora began to wonder if she could marry again. Not surprisingly, many of her acquaintances ridiculed this idea. "Why, Cora, a woman of your age!" exclaimed one. Another said: "Don't be silly, Cora. For God's sake, it's too late to be thinking about marriage! That's for young folk!"

But, as Alexander Pope so aptly put it: "Hope springs eternal in the human breast" and, as Tibullus said: "Hope ever urges on, and tells us tomorrow will be better." If Cora had anything going for her, it was her indefatigable hope. Though the derision of her friends sickened her at heart, still deep within her "human breast" was the light of hope that she, too, could still enjoy a married life with a loving man.

In defiance of all "logic" and "common sense," Cora began practicing *Psycho-Image Materialization*. Having fertilized the rich soil of her subconscious mind with *Psycho-Image Affirmation #5* and *New Miracle Dynamics Mind Activator #5*, Cora stolidly and perseveringly Psycho-Imaged herself to total and fulfilling joy in this life!

In the loneliness of her apartment, Cora began visualizing herself younger, lovelier, magnetic. She "pictured" a man near her own age coming to rescue her from this vale of tears. She "saw" herself attending a dance at a local club, and this tall, handsome, rich man came up to her and asked her to dance. He literally swept her off her feet, admired her greatly, couldn't stand to dance with any other woman but her, and by evening's end was hopelessly, totally in love with her. Cora reports:

"I spent a whole afternoon just Psycho-Imaging
this colorful, wonderful dream. I usually spend my
afternoons knitting or reading. But this day I

wanted to do something for myself, something constructive. I was simply tired of people telling me I
can't have happiness. Well, I guess I had recited the
Affirmation and the *Mind Activator* about four
times, and, lying comfortably on my sofa, I charged
my dream of joy and marriage with all the emotion I
really feel. I remember it was about 3:30 in the
afternoon—I'd been Psycho-Imaging my desires for
more than two hours—when someone knocked on
my door. I remember it bothered me, because I
didn't want to be disturbed: this was the most important thing I'd done in my life! When I opened the
door to chastise some interrupting friend, I stood
looking at this gray-haired man in a business suit.
He smiled and said, 'Hello, Cora. Maybe you don't
remember me. My name's Fred T. We met at a
dance a few months ago. We danced to *Till I Waltz
Again With You*. Do you remember?'

"With some effort I finally did remember, but
that was so long ago, so many dances ago! Then I
received the shock of my life. Standing there in the
hall, shifting from one foot to the other nervously,
Fred T. said, 'I know this will sound forward and
maybe ridiculous, but I haven't been able to get you
out of my mind since that evening. I've tried to
immerse myself in my work, I've even tried to push
you out of my mind. Today, coming here on a business deal, you seemed to fill my whole head. Cora, I
know this is strange, but . . . well . . . please come
out with me. Let me take you dining, dancing, club-
bing. I mean, well, you see, I . . . I think I'm in love
with you.'

"Talk about shocks! He was so personable, so sincere, so fervent! I was indeed swept off my feet!
One month later I married Fred—one month after
just two hours of *Psycho-Image Materialization*!
My dream had come true!

"Fred isn't as tall as the man I had visualized, but
he has a big heart. He isn't as handsome, but he's

kind and gentle and caring. He's not as wealthy, but he's the president of his own company and makes thousands more than my silly Social Security check! He isn't as daring as my dream-image, but he's forthright, honest, determined, and greatly respected in the business world. And I'm delirious with happiness!"

Happily married, Cora and Fred are enjoying their new life of harmony and bliss, though many said it couldn't be done! Fred had been, in fact, *created* by Cora! He was the living result of her own Psycho-Image, the one man who can fulfill her life, abolish her loneliness, and provide her with joy, money, position, and popularity—not to mention adoring, nurturing love! She had simply "put in her order" through *Psycho-Image Materialization* exercises and the Great Materializer provided what she needed!

Today, Cora has love, respect, honor, and, among all those doubters and scoffers she left in her dust, a certain amount of fame. Many of her former acquaintances are still trying to figure out how she did it!

How Psycho-Image Materialization Made Roger D. an Irresistible Lady's Man

Roger D. of Wheeling, West Virginia, worked in an office with a woman he greatly desired: Anita K. There was only one problem: Roger was neither handsome nor attractive and Anita had already made it quite clear that she wanted nothing to do with him. After all, Anita was ravishing, beautiful, and popular with many rich and handsome men. But Roger was hopelessly enamored of her beauty.

Anita had said one day: "Roger, if you bother me again, I'm going to have a friend talk to you." This was definitely a veiled threat of physical violence; Anita knew some men who were built like football players! But Roger could not turn off his feeling for Anita; it was bigger than he was. Defeated, frightened by her threat, Roger might have gone off to sulk and feel miserable or sorry for himself. He did none of these things. He practiced *Psycho-Image Materialization*. Like the water of *New Miracle Dynamics Mind Activator #5* that overcomes resistant materials, Roger doggedly persevered to overcome Anita's resistance. And his Psycho-Image exercise went to work immediately!

Having prepared his subconscious mind with the *Affirmation* and the *New Miracle Dynamics Mind Activator*, Roger began Psycho-Imaging even at his desk. Two days of this produced miraculous results. Roger relates: "I acted as if I were working, studying papers on my desk, but I wasn't. I was concentrating my mind on certain images, contacting superhuman forces to help me."

At the morning coffee break, according to Roger, he Psycho-Imaged Anita having coffee with him, even against her will. At the appointed time, he arose, went to her desk and said, "How about having coffee with me?" To which Anita replied, with glaring dark eyes, "No!" She turned away from him. But only for a moment. She suddenly turned back to him, her eyes soft. "Well, all right," she said.

At noon, Roger visualized Anita having lunch with him, and he saw in his mind's eye how she couldn't possibly resist him, couldn't say no, had to accompany him, obey him, yield to him. At a few minutes to twelve, he approached her desk. The conversation was brief, remarkable, mind-boggling.

"Lunch?" Roger asked. Just one word.

And Anita said one word: "Yes." He took her to lunch.

For the rest of the afternoon, appearing to work diligently at his desk, Roger was actually Psycho-Imaging that evening, that night. He pictured Anita succumbing to his charm, yielding to his desires. At five o'clock, he caught up with her at the door. "Dinner?" he asked. Anita looked at him uncertainly, as if she were somewhat confused in mind. "Well, I . . . yes, why not?" she finally said. Roger grinned triumphantly and took her by the arm.

During dinner, carrying on a conversation with the lovely Anita, Roger was at the same time already working on the next few hours, a crucial time as far as he was concerned. He was fervently Psycho-Imaging Anita in his arms, passionate, weak with desire, yielding, yielding, yielding. So charged with feeling and need were Roger's mental visions and so vulnerable to his mental force was Anita that at dinner's end all he had to say was: "Your place or mine?"

Without batting a lovely eyelash, Anita responded softly, "Mine."

Roger did not leave Anita's apartment until the following dawn!

This amazing episode was not followed by a long affair nor marriage. Roger explains it this way:

"I didn't realize the power at my disposal! I had been worshipping Anita as if she were a goddess, groveling at her feet, so to speak. But when *Psycho-Image Materialization* turned her into my own personal love-slave, I knew I didn't need her and her uppity ways. I went with her that one night and that's all. Heck, I discovered that this magic works with *all* women! I'm not saying I wouldn't have taken Anita out again. I might have. But, you see, there's this cute little blonde on the second floor. Her name's Candy. Mmm, is she candy! And then there's Judi in accounting and Karen in the stockroom and Alice on the switchboard and . . . well, there's also Lydia M., the boss's daughter! I just don't think I'm going to have time for Anita."

How New Miracle Dynamics Works Depends Upon Your Desires

Do you want to attract and command lovely, yielding women? Handsome, rich men?

Perhaps you require long-lasting love. Marriage? Social position? Honor? Respect? Fame?

We are all free to desire what we wish. No one has the right to condemn us for our choices or our life-style. Whatever you want is all right to want! Make up your mind, because once you start practicing *Psycho-Image Materialization*, you are going to get what you desire!

Formulate your desire. Recite *Psycho-Image Affirmation #5*. Recite it more than once, cultivating your subconscious mind. Reformulate your desire. Recite *New Miracle*

Dynamics Mind Activator #5. Then sit back and enjoy the fruits of your mental labor, for the Great Materializer, no respecter of persons, desires, or needs, will automatically activate in your outer life, attracting to you all you ever dreamed of and more!

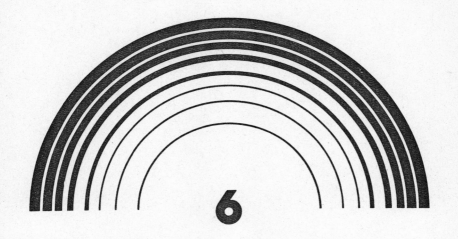

6

The Amazing Power
That Overcomes Enemies,
Combats Evil Thoughts, and
Dispels Negative Influences

None of us is entirely safe from enemies, evil thoughts, and negative influences. Let's face it: there are people in this world who are so reeking with animosity, hatred, and darkness that the more successful and happy you become, the greater are their efforts to undermine you, degrade you, and generally control your life. If you are a target of hatred, jealousy, envy, resentment or anger—be careful! Behind these so-called "human" emotions lie deep and insidious *psychic* powers that attack you, not on the physical level, but on the astral and mental levels! Have you ever been in the presence of a person whose mere proximity made your skin crawl or made you feel uncomfortable? That is psychic reality! And it is time you did something about it! Time you freed yourself from such invidious influence! Ignoring psychic attack is no defense against it: it may be secret psychic attack. What then? Then you need positive, constructive help— psychic help!

Psychic Attack Calls for Emergency Defense

Every reader of this book will discover in *Psycho-Image Materialization* techniques a guide and friend that will protect you from unseen but dangerous psychic attack. For the person who at last wants relief from this kind of subliminal influence, the remarkable technique presented here will provide you with the mystic knowledge that you will be able to ward off any and all such influences—quickly and easily! When you learn this sure-fire method of *Psycho-Image Materialization*, you will *never again* fall victim to hateful, spiteful, dangerous individuals. Thus, *Psycho-Image Materialization* becomes your emergency defense against psychic attack.

How Beatrice R. Was Being Slowly Vampirized by the Woman Next Door

Beatrice R., of Roanoke, Virginia, wrote recently that her next-door neighbor, one Ruth P., was so filled with jealousy that her emotions could be felt right through the walls of both houses!

Beatrice was a kind, understanding, helpful wife to her husband, a sympathetic, generous, nurturing mother to her children, a two-year-old boy and a four-year-old girl. She helped others whenever she could. She was known in the community as an altruistic, humanitarian person, and she was loved by all who knew her. By all but Ruth. Ruth, it seems, greatly envied Beatrice—envied her her home, her husband, her lovely children, her position in the neighborhood, even her looks, her money, her very life! Ruth was one mass of resentful, seething emotions that were invisibly but inexorably undermining the innocent Beatrice.

Beatrice explains that one day in January she fell incomprehensibly ill. She passed out while vacuuming the carpets! Just like that. When she came to, she found that her two children had been playing with matches: the bedroom was on fire! In the oven in the kitchen was a roast Beatrice had put on. For some inexplicable reason the fire went out but the gas remained on. Beatrice, screaming for help and trying to dial the phone with shaking fingers, heard a terrific explosion. The kitchen door came crashing into the living room! In just a matter of minutes, tragedy after tragedy manifested in this kind woman's life, scaring her practically to death. When policemen, firemen, and doctors arrived, all were saved from the disaster, but Beatrice had to be sedated and hospitalized. She was out of her mind with incomprehension and fear. All she could do was repeat again and again: "Why is this happening to me?"

Why indeed! Not a few yards away, watching Beatrice's house burn, was a grinning, evil-looking woman: Ruth!

How did Beatrice find out about Ruth? How did she combat this evil influence? What did she do to protect herself, her husband, and her children?

You will find the answer at the close of this chapter, along with the answers to two more terrible problems.

She Cried: "It Was Like Being Sucked Dry of My Blood!"

Witchcraft in twentieth-century America? Yes!

Sonya G., of New York City, is a living example of a young woman who was being cursed by a witch. Sonya had just come to New York from the small town in Iowa where she had been born and raised. Like many young women today, Sonya was single, independent, and looking forward with enthusiasm and youthful vigor to a bright new future. She arrived in New York, got herself a little apartment, even found a good job. She had everything going for her—except the friendship of one Diana L., a co-worker. Diana was into witchcraft and Black Magic, a believer in using dark forces for her own ends. She resented Sonya's simple beauty, and she hated the fact that Sonya had the job she wanted. So she decided to "get rid of Sonya" through nefarious means.

After only one week on the job, Sonya began to waste away—literally waste away. She was growing increasingly weak, thin, emaciated. Circles formed under her once pretty eyes. Age lines appeared prematurely on her smooth face. Her flesh yellowed and sagged. Her voice trembled when she spoke. Sonya sensed that something powerful and evil was eating away at her. Her friends began to avoid her, boyfriends ceased calling upon her, and she heard by mail that her brother had been imprisoned for rape and murder and that her mother had contracted cancer of the breast. Something "told her" that she must deal with this unseen force in an unseen way: doctors couldn't help, the police had nothing to go on, no one would believe her.

Sonya turned in desperation to *Psycho-Image Materialization*. And it worked miracles. See how below.

Why a Happy Groom Turned Into a Terrifying Monster

Barry M., of Ogden, Utah, was paradisiacally happy. He was moderately successful in his job, he was paying for his own home and, most of all, he was marrying the girl of his dreams, Nina T.

Two weeks after the wedding, as if in a nightmare, Barry

turned into an angry, wife-beating beast, he lost his job, his
home was taken from him for non-payment, he took to drink-
ing hard liquor daily, and his lovely wife Nina was paralyzed
with fear, dread, and a broken heart.

What created this horrible deterioration? One man! Sam
Y., living over 200 miles away from Barry and Nina, was a
former suitor of Nina's (she had turned him down as being too
coarse in manners) and was wishing the young couple nothing
but sadness, evil, trial, and horror! Sam's morbid anger and
jealousy was like a poison in his mind and, like a rock in a pool,
it was sending out dark ripples—even over a distance of hundreds of miles!

Only *Psycho-Image Materialization* saved Barry and
Nina.

The Mystic Secret of New Miracle Dynamics Saves You From Danger and Prevents Psychic Attack for All Time

Each of these unfortunate people used the very method
and technique you are learning right now. Beatrice used it,
Sonya used it, and Barry used it—to their undying relief!
Now you can use it. Even if you do not know of anyone's
deliberately trying to hurt or harm you, practice the following: an ounce of prevention is worth a pound of cure!

Psycho-Image Materialization Affirmation #6

*There is only one Mind, one Universe, one
God, and this Truth creates all Good in, through,
and around everything. The Living Spirit of God
fashions Right Action, Divine Order, and Perfect
Harmony at all times, in all places.*

*My mind is at-one with Universal Mind; there-
fore, only peace, tranquility, and serenity come
into my experience. As an expression of Infinite
Intelligence, no harm can come to me, no*

danger can threaten me, no enemy can assail me, no evil can vanquish me, no negative influence can defeat me, for in my mind and in Universal Mind these things have no life. All so-called negative influences, evil, darkness, and enmity are instantly dispelled in the Light that shines through my mind from Divine Mind, which is my Source and Protector.

Positive rays of Good overcome all evil in my life. My mind is radiant with darkness-destroying Light. I am suffused with protective, creative power, which emanates from me wherever I am to ward off and annihilate every kind of peril.

As my mind reflects and perpetuates Divine Mind, no negativity can touch me, hinder me, or interfere with my eternal happiness and well-being. All adversity, whether in the form of negative people, dark thoughts, or destructive influences, fall away like so much chaff before the swift scythe of protective Light.

With deep-felt gratitude I now acknowledge the Divine Source that has guided and protected me throughout my life and that I know will continue to guide and protect me from this day forward. "Yea, though I walk through the valley of the shadow of death, I will fear no evil." I rest securely in the hands of my Divine Protector, and I am thankful for this confidence. I go forth in life secure in the knowledge that no harm can befall me.

"Thou preparest a table before me in the presence of mine enemies: thou anointest my head with oil; my cup runneth over.

"Surely goodness and mercy shall follow me all the days of my life: and I will dwell in the house of the Lord forever."

I let it be so, and so it is!

Raise Your Vibrations to the Plane of Light-Beings and Then Activate Supernatural Power to Help You

Each of the stricken people mentioned above—Beatrice, Sonya, and Barry—used the foregoing *Affirmation* to raise their vibrations. Why? Because through the use of this *Psycho-Image Materialization Affirmation* you make contact with powerful Light Beings who have the force necessary to combat evil and negativity on its own level. As St. Paul put it: "The war is not against flesh and blood (physical people), but against principalities and powers of darkness (evil thoughts, feelings, and intentions)." The best way for you to fight non-physical influences is to have access to that level of being where other Light, non-physical forces operate. *Psycho-Image Materialization Affirmation #6* puts you in direct contact with this plane!

Once you have made contact, you are ready to employ the activator of those supernatural forces of Good.

New Miracle Dynamics Mind Activator #6

Psycho-Image three vital realities:

1. You and the Power of Light are ONE!
2. You are holding on in the face of adversity; you are pressing on to total victory.
3. LOVE defeats all evil; you are entertaining and maintaining nothing but Love-thoughts in your mind.

Here is the mystic secret to accomplishing this trio of power-influences.

For the first, say orally or mentally:

Power of Light, Power of Light
Give me energy, give me might.

Destroy my enemies, burn away fear
Stay with me always, stay near, stay near.

To activate supernatural agencies to help you attain the second power, say this:

No darkness shall stop me
No person, place, or thing;
I move forward victoriously
Peace and love to bring.

To attain the third power, say this:

LOVE is my power
Power from on high,
LOVE conquers all enmity
I will laugh, not cry.

These potent rituals will draw down supernatural help for you in times of trouble, conflict, or enmity. As you entertain dynamic Love-thoughts, your enemies automatically suffer the consequences of their own negativity, hatred, meanness, and anger. As Ella Wheeler Wilcox so aptly put it: "No matter how limited your sphere of action may seem to you, and how small your town appears on the map, if you develop your mental and spiritual forces through *love-thoughts* you can be a power to move the world along."

You need never entertain a negative thought against negative people, circumstances, or situations! All you have to do is recite the *Affirmation*, then use the rituals as outlined—and leave the rest to potent, psychic, supernatural powers! Bad people and conditions will fall away from you like magic!

They All Agree: "I Think I Would Have Died Without Psycho-Image Materialization"

Beatrice R., Sonya G., and Barry M. feel deeply that the above *Psycho-Image Materialization* exercises saved their lives!

When Beatrice started practicing the above techniques, an amazing thing happened. All the evil thoughts, negative influences, and perilous feelings emanating from her next-door neighbor *boomeranged* and afflicted their transmitter: Ruth P.! Beatrice immediately regained her health; Ruth was stricken with a dread disease. Beatrice renewed many new friendships; Ruth was left alone, as if she didn't exist. Beatrice rapidly recovered her dazzling beauty; Ruth looks three times her actual age. What is remarkable (and well worth your emulation!) is that Beatrice *never* held a bad thought for Ruth. On the contrary, she continually entertained *love-thoughts*! The evil backfired on Ruth on its own accord—or perhaps supernatural forces *sent* it back to its transmitter!

A similarly miraculous event occurred in the life of Sonya G. In her case, her enemy revealed herself. Diana, the practitioner of witchcraft and Black Magic, defiantly and proudly told Sonya to her face that it was she who was working evil forces in order to destroy Sonya. Sonya in turn took up *love-thoughts* through the practice of *Psycho-Image Materialization*. She envisioned Diana as a happy, successful, delighted, and delightful person! Two days later a "freak accident" occurred. Diana was walking along a street when a part of the concrete facade of a tall building gave way and hurtled to the pavement. Of all the people who were unsuspectingly strolling beneath the descending death-dealer, only Diana was hit! She was killed instantly, uncannily, unbelievably. And yet, Sonya had nothing to do with this evil woman's death; she merely cleared the psychic atmosphere of negative influence. The rest was out of her hands and in the hands of supernormal powers that regulate this universe.

As for Barry and Nina's terrible plight, all turned back into happiness once he began practicing *Psycho-Image Materialization*. In this case, Sam Y.'s evil thoughts did not boomerang (one never knows how supernatural forces will manifest, which is why it is written: "The Lord works in mysterious ways"). Rather, Barry's Psycho-Image exercises, in which he "pictured" his enemy well, happy, and receiving love, actually transformed a negative Sam into a positive Sam. You see, Barry's exercises and Psycho-Images sent out ripples of goodness to everyone (he did not know at the time just who was his enemy) and they surrounded and enfolded even Sam. He met and married a lovely woman, left off desiring Nina, and stopped feeling angry and hateful toward Barry. In short, Barry's Psycho-Image love-thoughts changed Sam! It was Sam himself, a few weeks later, who guiltily but forthrightly admitted to Barry and Nina by letter that he had been actively hating both of them. He apologized and begged their forgiveness. Barry and Nina forgot and forgave, and today both couples are the greatest of friends! Such is the miracle-working power of *Psycho-Image Materialization*.

How New Miracle Dynamics Gives You Fourth-Dimensional Aid and Protection Against Evil

Mystic masters throughout the ages have always taught their disciples that there exists in the fourth dimension a group of Spirit Protectors, an angelic order of Divine Beings under the rulership of Transcendent Masters, who spent their earth lives learning spiritual Truth and who now will help you if you ask for help.

The best way to ask for this Divine help is through your own subconscious, spiritual mind. Do this by practicing *Psycho-Image Materialization Affirmation #6*. You then activate your personal Spirit Guide by practicing *New Miracle Dynamics Mind Activator #6*. Remain restful and expectant. You do not know how your Guide will manifest in your life. Perhaps in dreams or in visions or in ideas or in thoughts— perhaps even physically! The angels in the Bible who appeared to Moses and Abraham and Lot—all these are extra-dimensional Spirit Guides—and some of them, you will remember, actually appeared in the flesh!

One thing is sure: Practice your *Psycho-Image Materialization* exercises diligently, and you need never worry about evil forces, dark people, negative circumstances, or undermining influences. You will go forth indomitable, unassailable, Divinely protected!

Psycho-Image Materialization Protects You From the Greatest Terror of All

Your *Psycho-Image Materialization* exercises will protect you from much more than has been so far discussed. As you experience Divine protection in your life, evading negative influences, overcoming evil, vanquishing sinister people, you also gain expertise to ward off the greatest danger of all: psychic warfare!

The world-famous Israeli psychic, Uri Geller, who performs mind-boggling feats of mental telepathy, ESP, and telekinesis (moving and bending objects with mental power), has sounded a warning we must all take seriously. In a recent article by Kathleen Thompson called "Mind Miraculous,"[1] Geller admits that he is afraid these powers may be used against us by our enemies. "The Russians are 50 years ahead of us in this kind of research," he says. "It is scary to think they may soon be able to turn a missile around or control the minds of our leaders."

Geller is right, of course. We must do all we can with our latent mind power to ward off this very real danger. As you develop your powers through *Psycho-Image Materialization* exercises, you become one of the few in this country to whom all can turn for real aid if and when that danger occurs! Bear in mind at all times that you can become a force for good. As Goethe said: "What you can do, or dream you can, begin it: Boldness has genius, power and magic in it."

Begin right now with *New Miracle Dynamics* to gain the

---

[1] Kathleen Thompson, "Mind Miraculous," *Science Mind*, March, 1978.

genius, power, and magic you need to combat insidious forces of negativity, evil, and destruction. In this time of peril, people all over the country are secretly developing their extra-sensory powers to do battle against enemy forces. You will be numbered among them as you practice PSYCHO-IMAGE MATERIALIZATION exercises and build up your psychic ability.

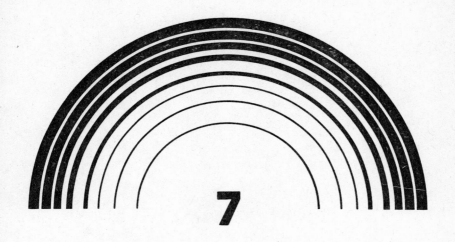

7

Million-Dollar Personality and Irresistible Charm Through Psycho-Image Materialization

How would you like every mind to acknowledge your presence when you enter a room? Have you ever noticed that one single person is the center of undivided attention at gatherings—in church, at the office, at parties? And have you noticed that this person is not necessarily attractive physically? You hear such statements as: "He's such a good conversationalist" or "she's such a wit" or "what a sparkling personality!" How would *you* like to be the one to elicit such encomium? How would *you* like to be praised, sought after, appreciated, valued?

Most of the statements you hear about "sparkling personalities" are references to *effects*. Have you ever noticed that the person lauded for his or her wit turns out to be not so witty after all? Have you ever noticed that the "beautiful" person really isn't a beauty at all? How do these individuals earn such lovely compliments? Why are they so attractive, so irresistible?

Learn this truth: *Charisma and charm attract people irresistibly, and charisma and charm are inner qualities!*

You cannot bottle charisma and charm. You cannot go to the store and buy some. No one else can give them to you. If you had a million dollars, you couldn't purchase these dynamic qualities.

And yet—charisma and charm will be *yours*! All you have to do is absorb the *Psycho-Image Materialization* secret to their acquisition and development. Once you do, *you will become the indisputable center of attraction wherever you go!*

And if that isn't reward enough, listen to this: it is the charismatic and charming personality who reaps a harvest of fringe benefits. The charismatic personality doesn't need a college education to succeed in business: his or her inner qualities of attraction *make* the individual a success! The truly charming person doesn't need money, fame, or notoriety to enjoy more fun and pleasure in life: his or her nucleus of attraction simply bears that person aloft into greater and ever greater circles of enjoyment! *You* will become that lucky person!

Since charisma and charm are inner qualities and not outer commodities, it follows that you must go inside to get them. What is "inside"? Your very own contact with superhuman agencies, the Source of these transcendent, indomitable forces that make others like you, support you, admire you, need you, and contribute their all to your health, wealth, success, and happiness!

The Psycho-Image Materialization exercise prepared here for you will make you a magnet for love, riches, friends, mates, aid, popularity, fame, good fortune, and countless other benefits. The first step toward your new life of excitement and popularity is the conscious preparation of your subconscious mind, much as the wise farmer cultivates his field in order to reap a harvest of good crops. Begin with this mind-clearing, obstacle-removing affirmation.

Psycho-Image Materialization Affirmation #7

Divine Mind is the Supreme Bestower of Beauty, Order, and Poise, as evidenced in our harmonious and beautiful cosmos. Choirs of angels sing praises to the Beauty which is called God, and this supernal quality of Attractiveness repeats Itself in all humanity.

As a being who is at-one with this Divine Source of magnetic Beauty, I embody, emanate, and express charm and charisma, unceasingly attracting to myself warm friends, passionate loves, and devoted companions. As the Sun is the center of this universe, so I am the center of my world, drawing to myself only the finest of people, the best of loves, the loveliest of partners. Everything unfolds from the center outward and I, too, discover my attractiveness occurring deep within my center and radiating

This is insoluble problem
So we cannot do
tha

Probing =

12 Gauge

Coveted =

<u>370 5409</u>

jibes =

1 883 683 6369

Candid =

1

Acquisition. การ บรรลุได้
การ ได้มา

In Soluble = บัสลายน้ำ Q = เเร
ไม่ ใช่

Insist = ยืนยืน

In Road = การได้ดี

Ghastly =

Adrenaline =

Charades =

Disperse = Go in different direction

Despise = Dislike Strongly.

???

into the world around me, acting at the same time as a powerful, irresistible magnet that attracts all good, help, love, respect, honor, and popularity.

I remain open and receptive to the infinite power of attraction in me, welcoming every wonderful person drawn to me. Every moment I become increasingly conscious of the attractive person that I am, and my expanded awareness of my uniqueness raises me to greater and greater experiences of popularity.

With a deep sense of gratitude I channel this magnetic Force that pulls admiring people into my world. I joyously accept the increasing numbers of friends, companions, and admirers, and I willingly give the glory to God. I am thankful for the Reality that I am a unique, attractive, charismatic, charming person, free of destructive self-concepts and free to enjoy, relish and cherish my new state of magnetism.

At this very instant there are people I do not yet know, but who are already feeling the pull of my attraction on the mental plane, people who will recognize me, aid me, uplift me, and admire me.

I know it is so, and so it is!

Attraction Is Mental but Its Benefits Are Material

Practice this Psycho-Image Materialization Affirmation until you *feel* its truth within yourself. Slow and mediative repetition will help you attain this requisite feeling, which in turn will establish your individual contact with invisible, transcendent Sources of magnetism. You will then channel these Forces, emitting them, radiating them, and drawing to yourself the realization of your dreams. Attraction, magnetism, and charisma are mental qualities, spiritual forces, if you will, but their results on this material plane are physical—fun, enjoyment, pleasure, riches, popularity, fame. The Cause is mental/spiritual; the effect or result is material/ physical.

Know that it matters not at all who you are, what you are, where you are, or what you want from helpful, higher-than-human forces. "God is no respecter of persons," says the Word, and this applies to you more than to any other person. You are getting in touch with cosmic reality, letting it come through you, operating on this earthly plane with fourth-dimensional force, inner force, potent force. Because you are doing this, you inevitably, inexorably emerge as an irresistible magnet for all that you want. People, luck, happy circumstances, beneficial conditions—all *must* come to you to help you *because* you are doing the excellent thing! You are incorporating transcendent powers into your being; therefore all good has no choice but to gravitate to you!

You are doing more than anyone else, so you will enjoy more than anyone else! It's that simple. By practicing the following Psycho-Image Materialization exercise, you are paving the road that will be inevitably traveled by helpful, loving people—right to you!

The woman who possesses inner poise and beauty attracts far more gallant and attentive men than the woman who spends a fortune on beauty parlors, cosmetics, and fashions. The man who possesses inner charisma and magnetism attracts more success and fame than the man who tries to "con" his way with a store of worldly know-how. When you channel the cosmic qualities of charisma and charm, you are irresistible—and here is the exercise designed to make you exactly that!

New Miracle Dynamics Mind Activator #7

Step 1: Cultivate the fertile soil of your subconscious mind with *Psycho-Image Materialization Affirmation #7*. Feel the transcendent power of universal magnetism coursing through your spirit, mind, and body. Permit this supernatural force to imbue your being. Let it flow into you, through you, around you. Let it exhilarate you; feel it throbbing, pulsing, pulling what you need and desire right to you.

Step 2: Activate and accelerate this mighty Power of the universe by repeating the *New Miracle Dynamics Mind Activator #7*. Your recitation will trigger and motivate this Power as surely as your ignition key starts the thrust of the engine in your car.

Step 3: Psycho-Image in living color. In a relaxed position, envision yourself being popular, irresistible, praised, wanted, and needed by everyone—or by that one special person you wish to recognize you. On the screen of your mind, see wealthy people helping you, giving you grand sums of money, promoting you in life, giving you fantastic breaks. Picture men (or women) drooling over you, craving your presence, your attention, your affection. Make your Psycho-Images vibrate with your need and desire, your feeling and expectation, your joy and anticipation.

Let your Psycho-Images be BIG! Remarkably beautiful women (or remarkably handsome men) surround you. At work you are inexpendable; you *must* be promoted; the boss has no choice but to pay you more, give you better jobs. At home your spouse finds you wise, kind, generous, so very much needed and appreciated. Your children, if you have any, respect you greatly, seek your qualified advice, long for your views on pressing problems, Your neighbors admire you, honor you, cannot help but visit you and listen to your advice. Strangers gravitate to you to help you, to be with you, just to hear your voice. Even enemies are transformed by your power into aiding, beneficial friends! Psycho-Image yourself as King (or Queen); all things, all people, all cir-

cumstances, all conditions are your footstool—
all geared to uplift and sustain you.

Step 4: Know beyond a shadow of doubt that
the Great Materializer will bring to pass in your
experience the joy and happiness and success
you deserve. Know that what you Psycho-
Image with feeling and faith will be materialized
before your very eyes—magically, invisibly, inexorably. If what you Psycho-Image does not materialize exactly as you pictured it, know that you
will receive something equal to or better than
that!

Your Psycho-Image Materialization Exercise Works Miracles and Produces Spectacular Results

Men and women everywhere get spectacular results in
their lives when they perform the preceding exercise diligently and in good faith. Attorney's secretary Linda F. simply wanted a raise in pay. The transcendent charm she chan-
neled so overwhelmed her employer that she lost her job—he
married her and took her "away from it all"!

Dan K., of Cleveland, Ohio, practiced *Psycho-Image Materialization* to attract a girl he liked. His new charisma is so
potent that he now rarely has a moment alone: women *hound*
him for dates. He reports with a grin: "I've been out every
single night for the past fourteen evenings—and not once
with the same girl twice!"

These are the kinds of miraculous transformations taking
place in many lives, and the same will happen to you. Perhaps
the most illustrative story, though, is that of Jane R.

How Psycho-Image Materialization Made Jane R.'s Life a Cinderella Story

Jane R. lives in a small town in Nebraska. Nothing very
much ever happened in her life. Confined to a little farm, the

only excitement she ever had came from television. Yet it was television that changed her life for all time, especially after she practiced *Psycho-Image Materialization*.

That Jane's life became a Cinderella story implies hardship—you will recall that Cinderella led a terribly hard life before the miracle freed her. Jane did not have a wicked stepmother. Sad to say, she had a "wicked" mother—and a wicked father! Both of Jane's parents were alcoholics. Now that didn't make them wicked, but their actions under the influence of alcohol did. Jane was a "battered child." Perhaps you have heard of these unfortunate children who are beaten and cruelly mistreated by unfeeling parents. Jane knows well, for she was systematically beaten for about eight years straight, whipped with a belt by her father and with an electrical cord by her mother. In spite of these adverse conditions, Jane practiced *Psycho-Image Materialization* with a passion—and it altered her life for all time!

One day, when she was 18, she was sitting and watching TV. At the end of the game show, a notice was flashed on the screen that anyone could write in and get tickets to see the show in person. Jane immediately Psycho-Imaged herself on the show, winning, winning, winning! She wrote for a ticket and received it a week later.

Terribly afraid of her parents, Jane "pictured" herself far away from her dire place, "seeing" herself in the audience of the TV show, laughing, enjoying herself.

What Jane did not know was that her Psycho-Image exercises—like yours—were activating Divine sources of help. They first gave her new excitement, new hope. Then they rippled out as they always do, and even as she lay Psycho-Imaging, miles and miles away forces were at work on her behalf.

In the wee hours of one morning, Jane said goodbye to the farm, to cruelty, to lovelessness. She hitchhiked all the way to California! "I never doubted for a minute that I'd have complete protection on my journey," she says confidently.

Jane achieved her goal, saw her dream come true. But there was infinitely more in store for Jane. Remember: When you Psycho-Image your desires, you activate superpersonal powers that may make manifest in your life things you never even thought of! The RIPPLES create new miracle dynamics!

Jane became a contestant on the show. She answered the first question. And won! Her prize was an electric range.

Question 2. Prize: a complete stereo system.

Question 3. Prize: a $3000 sailboat.

Question 4. Prize: a suite of furniture.

Question 5. Prize: $1000 in traveler's checks.

Question 6. Prize: a ten-day, all-expense-paid vacation in Hawaii.

Question 7. Prize: a wardrobe of her choosing.

Question 8. Prize: luggage.

Question 9. Prize: shoes, handbags.

Question 10. Prize: cosmetics.

Question 11. Prize: a color television

Question 12. Prize: a year's supply of gasoline.

Question 13. Prize: a brand new station wagon.

In less than 30 minutes, Jane R. accrued a total of more than $25,000! But that still isn't all. Jane was invited to another TV game show, then another, and another! Today, Jane does not work for a living. She is what we might call a professional contestant on game shows. Her winnings are astronomical:

- Morning game show, April: gifts valued at over $4500.
- Afternoon game shows, April: $55,000!
- Evening game show, April: $94,000!

Similar winnings accrued to Jane in May, June, July!

She also won a Jaguar, which she sports around Hollywood now, usually in the company of some handsome gentleman.

"I really feel just like Cinderella," Jane says now. "Magic

has happened in my life because of *Psycho-Image Materialization*. I've gotten so good at it that I can picture anything—and it comes to me! The most exciting part is that there is no pumpkin time, no midnight to end it all. It just goes on and on and on!"

And so it is! *Psycho-Image Materialization* activates miraculous powers to aid you, support you, sustain you, and generally enliven, lighten, and enrich your personal life. Jane today enjoys the popularity and charisma every girl should have.

How Barry L. Became a Popular, Happy Lady's Man!

Barry L., of Seattle, Washington, had a personal problem when I first met him. He said, "All I want is some female companionship. But I'm not good-looking or rich or popular. What can I do? Can *Psycho-Image Materialization* help me find love and friendship?"

Of course it can. It can do anything you let it. I told Barry so. I told him to go home, get quiet with himself, mentally recite the *Affirmation*, use the *Mind Activator*, and "picture" himself dancing with scores and scores of beautiful women.

Barry started his Psycho-Image program on a Tuesday. On Sunday following he called me and said, "I'm reeling! I can't believe this! All of a sudden I'm fantastically popular!"

He told me his story this way:

> "I was walking down to the store the other day and this young woman came up to me and asked me for a date! She said she's one of the new kind of females who like to take the initiative! She saw me going to the store and decided to approach me. The next thing I knew, her girlfriend wanted a date with me. Then her friends. Believe it or not, I'm all booked up for the next solid week!"

And that's how it happens when the ripples fan out! These women say there is "something" about Barry that they can't resist. And isn't that what it's all about, "something"? Call it what you will: charisma, charm, magnetism, whatever. You can have the same fun and enjoyment that Barry has!

How Cindy F. Won the Man She Wanted Most

Cindy F. lived alone in Cleveland, Ohio. She was leading what she described as "an unbearably lonely life." Then she started practicing *Psycho-Image Materialization*. In her Psycho-Imaging, she "saw" herself loving the man she wanted most. And here's the miraculous part: the man was already married! Then, why did Cindy do it? She says:

> "While Jim was at work, his wife was cheating on him day in and day out. He's a kind, wonderful man and doesn't deserve that kind of cruelty. One day he and his wife had a terrible fight. They split up. I was already Psycho-Imaging myself as his loving, understanding, compassionate wife. When he came by and asked me for a date, I almost fell over, but in my heart I thanked God for this wonderful event. My Psycho-Imaging worked a miracle in my life!"

Cindy is not lonely today. She and Jim are married, and there is a little one on the way. They are supremely happy with each other.

Cindy says: "I think any lonely woman should use *Psycho-Image Materialization* to win the heart of the man she wants. Maybe you could pass on to others the chant I used."

I told Cindy I would do so, and here is the chant that she used during her Psycho-Image exercises:

> *I am a loving, helpful person*
> *Feel my love, O man who needs me;*
> *May my love ripple through walls*
> *To touch your heart and make you mine!*

She Was Unmarried Because She Thought She Was Drab

The above case reminds me of Diana L. of Ogden, Utah, a slim woman who had a terrible opinion about herself. She thought she was drab! It is remarkable how we grow up seeing ourselves as *others* told us we are! You are not what others think of you! Diana learned this through the use of *Psycho-Image Materialization* exercises. She found out that you can be whatever you want to be! PICTURE IT! Believe in the picture of yourself! And thank God *before* the miracle happens!

Diana "attuned" her subconscious mind by reciting the *Affirmation* and using the *New Miracle Dynamics Mind Activator*. That's always the first step! Then she chanted:

> *Miracle-working Power above*
> *Enter my life*
> *Produce in this person*
> *Beauty and charm.*
> *Wonder-working Power above*
> *Hear my call,*
> *Charisma I want*
> *Aura and all.*

The secret is the "aura." Beauty is only skin deep, but your aura of beauty, deep and lasting, is what really attracts the opposite sex! Diana is now deliriously, happily married. She says: "I'm happy now because I permitted inner and cosmic forces to transform me into a charismatic person, supremely attractive to men."

Remember that *Psycho-Image Materialization* also works for men. Attune yourself with the *Affirmation* and the *Mind Activator* and then use your power of "picturing" to see yourself as you want to be, getting whatever you want.

How New Miracle Dynamics Increases Your Popularity

Psycho-Image Materialization Opens your subconscious mind to the influx of energy, vitality, and vigor, thus transforming you into a personable, charismatic, auric personality. With constant practice you will tap higher powers that will change your looks, your personality, your sex appeal, and your popularity.

Follow the instructions in this chapter, and each day check yourself in the mirror. Notice anything different? *You will!*

Attune your mind, say some of the chants provided for you in these pages, and *thank higher powers prior to receipt*!

Then sit back and watch the amazing, exciting, life-fulfilling miracles take place around you!

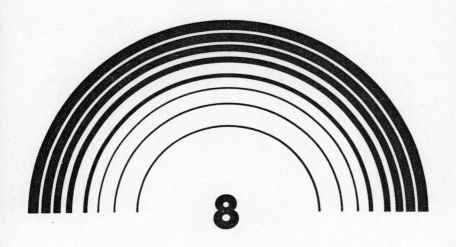

8

Let Psycho-Image Materialization Magnify Your Personal Success Rate

Many centuries ago, men and women in the far corners of the earth knew the ancient secrets of the Universe. You have heard of these workers of magic: they could make plant life grow miraculously, turn lead into gold, command obedience from others, heal people supernaturally, repel enemies, stop storms, produce food seemingly out of thin air. They could do many wondrous things. What was their secret? Magic words? Miraculous rituals? Secret traditions? I'd like to share their secret with you right now.

The Secret to Magical Power Is No Secret to You!

You have read stories or seen films about magic wands, pearls, stones, amulets, and a host of other objects. Let me ask you a simple question: If you saw a magician right now produce a rabbit out of a hat by touching the hat with a magic wand, where, would you think, lies the magic, in the man or in the wand?

Think about it! You see what I'm getting at, don't you? The wizard, the magician, the witch, the god, the guru, the healer—each of these *human beings* had initimate contact with higher-than-human forces. Didn't they?

I think you know as well as I do that if you possessed the magician's wand, it would in no way guarantee that you could then work magic. Why not? If you had the elixir of life and drank it, you would not have eternal life. Why not? If you unearthed a great secret ritual used by fifteenth-century witches, it won't work today. Why not?

Here's the secret: Magical things, objects, talismans, amulets, wands, formulas, and incantations are only as powerful as *you* are!

Here's another secret: All workers of magic, past or present, did not have magical "things," but magical *contact' with superpersonal power.*

Psycho-Image Materialization is *your* key to contacting and implementing this Universal magical force. This book imparts to you the *means* by which "things" become magical. Through the keys, secrets, and formulas outlined in this book, you will achieve the *state of mind* that was (*had to be*) shared by all saints, wizards, magicians, and healers. The fact is that these marvelous workers of miracles were men and women just like you and me! No different, except for their transcendent state of mind. With that state of mind, nothing could be denied them. If they wanted love, they got love. If they wanted money, they got money. If they wanted success, they got success. Now you can do the same!

In ages past, our modern terms simply weren't available. Without going into ancient terminology, it is safe to say that the miracle-workers of days gone by used Psycho-Image Materialization to produce the things and the joys and the successes they desired. They were able to use the power of mind to produce materiality out of immateriality. So can you! Why? Because no matter what vast changes have taken place down through the centuries, the Mind used then is the Mind you are using now! Your dress is different, your needs are different, the age in which you live is different, but, believe me, my friend, you have access to untold power. All you have to do is learn how to tap it, channel it, store it. And this book will show you how. I know scores of men and women—once suffering human beings—who now enjoy phenomenal and miraculous success in life because they learned how to use Psycho-Image Materialization.

How Don L. Used Psycho-Image Materialization to Rise Above a Financial Crunch that Others Still Suffer

I met Don L. in Eureka, California. He was down and almost out. He was living with friends like a dependent, no money in his pockets, and was out of work for seven months when I met him. He needed help desperately and wanted to know how he could change his poverty into riches and success. We went to a local coffee shop and talked for more than an hour, during which time I told him about Psycho-Image Materialization and the dormant powers of his mind.

"Can you help me?" he asked. "I'm tired of taking handouts from people who love me. I want to be financially independent. I can't get a job. I'm wearing the last of the few clothes I have. I'd like a place of my own, a car, and a refrigerator full of food. I don't know; maybe I'm asking too much. People all around me are out of work. Things are getting worse and worse."

"Hold on there," I replied to this negativism. "You're so busy seeing lack and limitation that you're setting up subconscious blocks to your own success! You have to affirm your own plenty in the face of apparent lack. Why don't we begin with an affirmation that will instill in you a healthier realization of your own success potential? Let's get you on your feet."

I gave Don a Psycho-Image Materialization Affirmation and asked him to use it for a week, just to help clear his befogged mind of negativism and to prepare it for new, more hopeful activation.

He used the affirmation daily, faithfully, and when I saw him next, I gave him a Psycho-Image Mind Activator. Both the affirmation and the activator were geared to bring this poor man instant and miraculous success—even as others continued to suffer deprivation and limitation.

A week later Don met me once again at the coffee shop. But he didn't walk there this time. He drove up in a brand new Jeep (something he'd always wanted to own), and he was wearing spiffy new clothes. He'd even had his hair cut and styled. He looked like a million!

"I feel like a million!" was his first outbreak of joy, grinning ear to ear. Then he told me about the miracle in his life. "I used the secrets you gave me and overnight things began to happen! I've had work applications out, you know? Heck, I forgot about half of them. I figured I'd never get any of the cushy jobs I applied for. But, guess what! I received a phone call the other day and in ten minutes—over the phone!—I was hired as a sales manager for a big outfit in San Francisco!"

Breathlessly, excitedly, he went on. It's always a delight

to see someone flushed with success. "That's where I just came from," he laughed. "San Francisco. I'm going to live there, work there and—" he chuckled "—*love* there! You know why? I wasn't in that big, beautiful office five minutes, waiting to see the big man, when this gorgeous secretary struck up a conversation with me. She clued me in on some things I ought to know about and things I should mention during my interview. She told me how to present myself to the boss, whom she knew better than me. And it worked! But later, when I came back out, she asked *me* if I wanted to take her to lunch. One of those new women, you know? Well, I hid my embarrassment and said heck, yes, I'd take her to lunch. I'd take a beautiful woman like that anywhere she wanted to go!"

He paused to catch his breath and before I could congratulate him on his good fortune, he continued exuberantly: "We're dating, Sheila and I, and Mr. Phillips, the boss, is sure I can do the job for him. Got my own office, I had no trouble finding a neat bachelor pad and—best of all Mr. Laurence!—my salary is $75,000-a-year! What can I say? I'm speechless! Yesterday a bum, today a rich man—with love, a home, a car, clothes—everything! How can I ever thank you?"

"No need to thank me," I said. "The whole idea behind Psycho-Image Materialization is to get people like you started on a more fruitful, pleasurable life, and when it happens, that's reward enough for me. After all, I use it myself, you know!"

What Don Did, Anyone Can Do— Especially You

Don had no magic wand, no secret spell, no potent formula. And yet it is *as if* he did! He had what makes magical objects effective: an awakened, activated mind, the mind of the magician! You can do as he did and turn any lack or limitation around for yourself. However you can conceive of success, it is at your fingertips right now—in spite of appearances to the contrary. Actually, the greater you suffer, the more chance you have of ending that suffering. People who are not suffering are not growing, nor are they asking for help. "Ask and you shall receive," as the Master put it. It has been my limited experience that men and women who have endured suffering with patience and perseverence (keeping the faith) are amply rewarded by practicing Psycho-Image Materialization.

You have suffered enough (not to mention Don and a thousand other successful people) and I want to share with you what works in this time of economic stress. If you want to turn dearth into plenty, begin with the following technique.

Psycho-Image Materialization Affirmation #8

Life is not something that happens to me by mere chance; I create my life day by day with my thoughts. My mind molds the Life-force into whatever I wish; therefore I will Psycho-Image good things for myself and watch them materialize in my outer awareness.

I am grateful for all the success and happiness that is mine—even before it manifests—for my success is the expression of the Life-force working through me, as me, for me. The lack and limitation seen by those around me no longer has any effect on my life. Dearth and success are self-created; I therefore Psycho-Image success for myself.

I know that success is a continuous flow of conditions and circumstances that are plastic in my mind. I realize that my Psycho-Images mold outer appearances to make my life more abundant, and I am grateful for this ancient truth. I accept my success here-and-now, knowing on faith that it is my own creation as miraculous Life-force courses through me.

I know that the Universe is made up of abun-

> *dance. I live and move and have my being in this*
> *abundance. Since there is nothing but success*
> *in the Universe, there is nothing but success in*
> *my life. Every facet of my life, every area in my*
> *life, every condition and circumstance is right*
> *now moving to increase my good, my richness,*
> *my plenty. And I am now grateful.*
>   *I* command *success with gratitude!*

Affirm, Open, and Get Ready to Receive More Than You Asked For!

Bear in mind that Don L. had only the above Affirmation and one Activator to work with, while you have a whole book full! Yet he received more than he dreamed possible! Think about this! What Don did, you can do, and more!

It is not an idle statement when I tell you the well of success has no bottom. Limitless supply is yours for the asking—if you know how to ask. Repetitive prayers are not the secret, as the Gospels show. Much prayer avails nothing. But to have the mind of Christ—ahh, that's another story! *Then* you will receive all you need, desire, wish, and more, much more. Once you open the floodgates of abundance with your Psycho-Image Materialization Affirmation, there is no telling the wonders you will behold. One thing is certain: you will be filled, happy, enriched, successful!

A Few Simple Rules For Getting the Most Out of Your Psycho-Image Materialization Affirmation

Sit or lay down comfortably. "Untense" yourself. Relax. Be comfortable. Let your eyelids close slowly about halfway.

Prop this book so you can scan the page easily. If you hold it in your hands, do so gently, not tensely. Read the affirmation through several times. Let it sink into your subconscious mind.

Then you are ready to implant the Psycho-Image Mind Activator into your prepared brain-soil. Before you do so, take a few minutes to entertain thoughts of exactly how you would like success to manifest in your life. See yourself doing the wonderful things you really want to do. Visualize yourself *enjoying* success. Do not see yourself overcoming obstacles or setbacks—the Life-force galvanized by your Psycho-Images will overcome all blocks to your success.

When you think you are ready, implant this powerful activator:

New Miracle Dynamics Mind Activator #8

1. Materialize success-force by taking six deep breaths. With each inhalation, Psycho-Image powerful energy being drawn by you from the outer reaches of the cosmos. Picture this energy imbuing you—mind, body and spirit—completely enfolding you.

2. Picture yourself thoroughly imbued with and completely enclosed in this cosmic energy.

3. Imagine this force-field to be a powerful magnet, attracting to you and only you all the wonderful things you desire.

4. Now command (with gratitude beforehand!) this force. Mentally compel the cosmic power to help you by thinking in this way:

   I command *success to manifest in my life as* _____ (Insert your desire).

Once you have formulated your desire in a clear Psycho-Image, it will materialize as if by magic. Give no thought to how it will manifest or through whom. By no means should you wonder

---

how such a miracle can possibly occur for you. This is doubt! Keep the faith, use the affirmation and the preceding activator with complete sincerity and expect it to work! It will!

After you have employed the Psycho-Image Mind Activator, be grateful immediately, for you have worked the miracle already in mind. Everything begins in mind. Look about you. Everything you can see, from ashtrays to tables to television sets, were all once ideas in someone's *mind*—then they became manifest as physical realities. So it is with your success.

How success comes to you is not your concern. Someone may pick up your command by mental telepathy and fulfill your needs. You may win a contest. Expect your Psycho-Imagery to work in a quick, easy, and miraculous way. You will be as delighted as Don L. was, as happy as scores of people are who use these potent techniques.

Her House Caught Fire, Her Car Blew Up, and She Wanted to Die

I met Doris P. of Roseville, California, through my friend Jim, who runs a suicide prevention center. Jim, by the way, got involved in this kind of work when Psycho-Image Materialization programs helped him so much that he wanted to help others.

When I first saw Doris, she looked haggard, worn out, lost, and defeated. I listened to her story and soon learned why the poor woman was on the brink of suicide. For one thing, she'd lost her husband in Viet Nam. She was supporting two small children alone.

"It hasn't been easy," she said to Jim and me, with tears welling in her eyes. "But I've been doing pretty good as a waitress. I've been making the house payments a little late, but I've been making them. Things were looking a mite better recently. I was even able to buy Becky—that's my youngest—a new dress this month. Then—then—"

We waited as Doris broke into tears. I gave her my handkerchief and she dried her face after a few minutes.

"I'm sorry," she sniffled, "but I just don't know what I'm going to do. As you know, I put my head in an oven to kill myself. I'm so ashamed about that. To think I would have abandoned my children that way, feeling sorry for myself. But I couldn't think straight after what happened."

What had happened was this: One afternoon while Doris was at work (and the children were with friends on the other side of town, thank God!), something blew up in the cellar of their home. In just moments the entire house was engulfed in flames. Since the garage was attached to the house, it too caught fire, and Doris's car (she'd gone to work by carpool that day) blew up. It was a terrible explosion, heard for miles around. By the time Doris reached this part of her story, she was sobbing.

"Everything we owned went in that fire," she cried. "All the kids' clothes. Even Becky's new dress. Our furniture, my keepsakes from my dead husband, the few dollars I was saving to send Billy on a camping trip—everything went up in smoke. And now I feel absolutely finished. I wanted to die."

Jim gave me a glance that said he thought I might be of some help to this pitiful woman. He left the room and I talked with her for some hours, reminding her of the incredible truth that no matter how dark the night, the day is always bright with God's sunshine. I reinforced her dwindling faith in herself, reminded her of her responsibility to the children, reawakened an expectation of good things in her.

When I thought she was ready, I told her about Psycho-Image Materialization and shared the good news that she still had the most precious thing in the world: her mind.

"If you will use your mind as the magical tool it is," I said, "I think you will find miracles happening to you. There's no need to give up now. I know how you feel, but believe me, I know people who are worse off. I know a man who just lost his legs in a car accident, a woman who is dying of cancer, and yet both of them are right now enjoying this life and all its successes. So will you."

I gave her the Psycho-Image Materialization Affirmation and the Mind Activator. She'd said she was willing to try anything to bring happiness into the life of her children. I suggested she use the techniques outlined for you in this chapter. And she did.

That very day Doris Psycho-Imaged the success-producing energy-field around herself and imagined it around her children, too. I impressed upon her that no one could predict how the materialization would take place. You see, she had started to worry about that.

"But a house!" she cried. "How can I get a house? And all our clothes, hundreds of dollars worth!"

I nipped this kind of worry in the bud. "Use the affirmation dozens of times," I told her. "It will help you to stop looking at impossibilities and to begin seeing the possibilities. All things are possible."

I left her alone with the Psycho-Image techniques that you now have before you. I went and talked outside with Jim for an hour or so. During this time the miracle occurred—the same afternoon!—that reduced Doris to tears once again—this time tears of joy!

She Psycho-Imaged Her Success, and It Came to Her Within Four Hours!

A huge black Cadillac pulled to the curb in front of Jim's establishment. A man came in, well-dressed, with diamonds on his fingers. He introduced himself as Cary F. and showed us his business card.

"I understand the woman whose house burned down is here," he said. "May I see her, please?"

Jim and I escorted the man into the other room, and he immediately gave Doris a friendly hug and expressed his regret over her terrible misfortune. I already sensed at that point that Doris's Psycho-Imagery was materializing. It was—in a big way!

To make a long but beautiful story short, Cary F. turned out to be an active philanthropist, a man dedicated to helping the underprivileged. I have since learned that he's a millionaire three times over.

His intention was quite clear. Smiling benignly at the wide-eyed Doris, he said, "Please accept what little help I can give you in your time of stress. I understand you have two small children also. Let me help you."

He used the phone, made four authoritative calls, and in a flash, as it were, had Doris and her children living in a plush motel. He ordered plenty of food for them. He ordered them a rented car and paid for its use. He called a large department store and ordered all sorts of clothing for Doris and the kids.

But that was just the beginning. That was just one day's miracles! About a month later, I received a call from Doris—a new, vibrant, deliriously happy Doris.

"Oh, Mr. Laurence!" she enthused. "I don't know how to tell you this. Mr. F. has been so kind. You know all about that. What you don't know is that he has asked me to marry him! Yes, me! He loves my children, and he said that now that he's been with me, he can't live without me! And I owe it all to you!"

"No, you don't," I laughed. "You owe it to yourself for not killing yourself, for trusting in things not seen, and for practicing Psycho-Image Materialization with complete faith. I told you no one could predict how it would make itself manifest. I'm delighted that Cary wants to marry you, but I'm not surprised that your Psycho-Imagery has made itself manifest in a fast, easy, and miraculous manner."

Today Doris is a very busy hostess in her palatial home in Beverly Hills—a home, by the way, that is worth ten times as much as the house that burned down. Her Psycho-Imagery paid off big. Now she not only has a new house and happy children, but a loving, kind, altruistic husband besides!

Such miracles are commonplace in the lives of men and women all over the country who utilize the powers of Psycho-Image Materialization.

You can enjoy the same or similar joys!

9

The Secret Force That Puts You in Command at All Times

Why abolish inferiority? Why establish self-confidence?

Have you ever heard of an inferior magician? An inferior god? An inferior charismatic person?

Have you ever heard of a miracle-worker who suffers lack of confidence? What do you think would happen to a snake charmer, for instance, if he suddenly felt that he didn't have what it takes to charm the snake? Or to a lion tamer suffering an inferiority complex?

Simply put, inferiority undermines your chances at superior living; self-confidence makes you radiate success and happiness! Inferiority makes you weak and helpless; self-confidence creates a new, vibrant you! Power like Psycho-Image Materialization remains a mere idea; in the hands of a person glowing with self-confidence, it creates miracles!

You will need self-confidence to employ Psycho-Imagery successfully, as you will see in the next chapter: "How to Control Thoughts and Feelings with New Miracle Dynamics." No one lacking self-confidence can command others! With self-confidence you can create a world of happiness, fruitfulness, and joy!

If you will practice the program outlined in this chapter for your betterment, you will avail yourself of such potent life-enhancers as:

- Verve
- Optimism
- Vigor
- Self-reliance
- Boldness
- Courage
- Certainty
- Power
- Might
- Energy
- Enthusiasm
- Hope
- Ardor
- Spirit
- Faith
- Security
- Assurance
- Potency
- Strength
- Authority

And this will be but the beginning!

How to Become Super Confident—and Stay that Way!

Until self-confidence is a reality, each man, woman, and child is a body with a mind, an object to be manipulated and influenced by outside forces: environment, heredity, habits, imposed ideas, beliefs and opinions, the actions and reactions of others. Yet you have the potential to affect, use, control, neutralize, or depotentiate these forces by learning *how to* through the use of Psycho-Image Materialization and then applying your new principles to convert your potentiality into real and present power!

I am fully convinced today that with all the negative social influences with which we are faced—*fear* of poverty, *fear* of failure as men and women, *fear* of enemies, *fear* of unemployment, *fear* of inflation, *fear* of dishonesty in high places—the time is at hand for people like you and me to start creating our own success and happiness.

Do you have one or more of these fears? Good! Here's why I say good: *In every human, fear is a seed of equal or greater confidence for those who apply Psycho-Image Materialization secrets.*

Begin right now to attack the source of the fears, anxieties, and inferior feelings that undermine you.

Here for your benefit and for all-time use is the secret to super confidence, beginning with a potent affirmation to eradicate inferiority in you.

Psycho-Image Materialization Affirmation #9

Aware that all my life experiences begin in my thought, I banish all fear from my mind. I fear nothing, no one, because I do not recognize as real any thought that denies the power, worth, love, or importance of me. My awareness of the truth of me banishes fear of all things from me.

Adversity does not scare me; it instills in me the will to succeed.

> *Setbacks do not deter my progress; they fire me up for greater achievement.*
> *Negative people do not intimidate me; they show me what I do not want to be.*
> *Inflation does not worry me; it creates a powerful hunger in me for more, which I will satisfy.*
> *Enemies do not intimidate me; they encourage me to be stronger than they are.*

How a Salesman Used Psycho-Image Materialization to Overcome His Self-Defeating Inferiority

A few months ago, I visited a salesman who was very ill. There was nothing organically wrong with the man. He was suffering one of the most serious diseases I know of: demoralization. He had once been a promising salesman, when all the breaks were in his favor, but the time had come for him to use his own latent powers, and the poor man had no idea what these were, much less how to employ them! Consequently, he felt the world was against him, that his usefulness as a breadwinner had come to an end. Life became tasteless and fruitless for him. Sales dropped off considerably, even though he could not see the connection between his state of mind and outer reality. He did not know that his sense of inferiority was destroying him, mind, body and soul, as well as socially, financially and personally.

At that time I appealed to his sense of self-worth. "You tell me things were once going well for you," I said. "Good! Be thankful for that, and don't bewail its passing. Self-pity will get you nowhere. You were once confident in yourself. What happened? And don't tell me the breaks went against you. If you will be rigorously self-honest right now; you will find the real culprit deep inside yourself."

He thought. He dropped his head into his hands and searched inwardly. And he came up with the real answer to his own problem.

"You're right," he said. "This whole slump began when I had to sell our product to a millionaire. I just couldn't go through with it. I mean, look at me! Who am I to be setting up an interview with a man like that? His suite of offices was enough to turn me around and send me packing."

The switch from self-pity to self-honesty did the trick. I simply gave him Psycho-Image ammunition to work with.

"Can you picture this rich man as a chimpanzee?" I asked. "Just imagine yourself in his office and, instead of the overbearing, intimidating image you have of him, see him as a lovable chimp behind his big desk. Can you do that?"

My friend burst into laughter. "Yes, yes," he chuckled, sighing a huge sigh of relief (laughter is good for the soul), "I can see him that way!"

"Fine," I said. "Then you are on your way. Get rid of old ideas about power and authority. You'll go broke in no time if you let your images of people, places, and things intimidate you and scare you."

He practiced the above affirmation for seven days. Then I gave him the Mind Activator that follows. He practiced that for seven more days. Then he went to see the ominous millionaire and sold him the goods!

In short, this man turned poverty into riches in just two weeks time. He came away from the luxurious suite of offices with a contract worth $40,000!

What he accomplished, you can accomplish, and in the very same way. Your circumstances may be different. Conditions may be different in your case. But we all share one thing in common—our humanity. The millionaire is a human being, the salesman is a human being, I am a human being, and you are a human being. Strangely enough, we forget about this commonality. We tend to see self-defeating images around us and we are afraid. Nonsense! *Picture it! See* what you want. *Change* your images of people, places, and things with Psycho-Imagery and go forth conquering!

New Miracle Dynamics Mind Activator #9

When you think someone is "too important" to bother with you; if you believe a certain man or

woman is "too good" for you; when you believe
you are not worthy of love, wealth, success, happiness, romance, friendship—or a million other
good things in this life—STOP! Stop and use the
Psycho-Image Materialization Affirmation provided for you in this dynamic chapter. Then employ this miracle-working technique:

1. Psycho-Image the "other" (whether person, place or thing) in an outrageous form.
   Be liberal in your imagery. Let your subconscious formulate a new image to relate to.
   One man was afraid to approach a remarkably beautiful woman because she
   looked so sure of herself, so assertive, so
   "with it." He Psycho-Imaged her as a helpless female dying with love for him, aching
   to meet him. It worked!

2. Psycho-Image yourself in a similar fashion.
   The man I just mentioned pictured himself,
   not as unworthy of a gorgeous woman's
   love, but as the very man she was *waiting*
   for!

3. Understand once and for all that when you
   look at people, places, and things, you are
   in a sense looking into a mirror. You are
   looking at images, not things as they really
   are. Many brash and even rude people are
   actually hiding feelings of insecurity and
   inferiority. You can capitalize on this
   through your use of Psycho-Imagery. Destroy false images (idols!) with your powerful mind! Begin with your own.

4. Stand before your mirror daily. The image
   you see is little different from the images
   you see in the "mirror of life." And you can
   change them! If you will begin with your
   own image, you will accrue a great wealth
   of experience and will then be able to alter
   intimidating, defeating images around you

at will. Look in your mirror and see yourself as you *want to be*, not as you think you are or as others say you are. Here's the inner secret: *You are already who you want to be—you simply don't know it!* Practicing the principles of Psycho-Image Materialization will help you to KNOW! Each day say this:

> *I am* _____ (place a strong adjective in this space, such as "beautiful," "rich," "powerful," "irresistible," "potent," etc.). *I am a tremendous success, filled with confidence and vitality. I am attractive to everyone, to the same sex because they would like to be as I am, to the opposite sex because they need a person like me. I am loved. I am loving. I exude confidence, enthusiasm, vigor, and beauty. I am a magnet—a human magnet—for health, wealth, success, and happiness. Harmony surrounds me and manifests wherever I am. Peace and tranquility are mine. I am happy, joyous, loving, and kind, and no one, male and female, can resist my charm and personality.*

Jill S. Was a Loser Until She Practiced Psycho-Image Materialization

Jill S. of Scranton, Pennsylvania did exactly as I have told you in this chapter. You see, she was a loser, by her own admission. At 19 years of age, she was still living with ("off of," she put it) her parents. She was afflicted with a horrible case of psychosomatic acne (caused by negative images of herself), which disfigured her face. So she was a frightened, unsocial person, afraid to date, afraid to get out in the world, afraid to live alone, afraid to find work for herself.

Jill's unfounded fears only contributed to her illnesses and setbacks and obstacles to her happiness. Sick and tired of being sick and tired, she started using the self-help program outlined in this book for you. And miracles occurred in her life so rapidly that they took her breath away.

1. Her acne completely disappeared, as if by magic. One day as she stood before her mirror to practice her Psycho-Image Mind Activator (she had been picturing herself as completely beautiful), the ugly marks and pimples vanished right before her eyes! Just as the human body has the capacity to deteriorate by subconscious command, so it has the power to heal itself by the same principle!

2. A girlfriend asked Jill to accompany her to the store. Jill bumped into a tall, dark-eyed, handsome man who redeemed the embarrassing collision by grasping her shoulders, looking deep into her eyes and saying, "I've been looking for you all my life." Barriers of self-deprecation fell away like scales. The man asked her for her phone number. She gave it to him. Today they are loving partners in their own business, which nets each of them $50,000 per year!

3. Jill has a date book that would turn any woman's eyes green with envy. She keeps a photo album of her men, 10″ × 12″ glossies of sexy, smiling, charismatic males who adore her!

She wrote to me recently:

"It's a miracle! There's no stopping the wonderful things happening in my life now. Once I began practicing your Psycho-Image program, nothing has been like in the old days. Inferior? I don't even know the meaning of the word! I just get up every morning and express gratitude out loud for whatever will happen in my life this one day. I live one day at a time now and each and every day is filled with wonder for me. I'm so happy!"

Psycho-Image Materialization Demonstrates That What Imprisons You Will Set You Free—If You Let It!

You can do as others are doing every day with Psycho-Image Materialization practices. Bob R., of Chico, California, didn't think his artwork was worthy of anyone's serious admiration. He tried the techniques outlined in this chapter, and a month later he won an art scholarship! His own dream came true in thirty days!

Cindy F., of Orlando, Florida, thought she was condemned to a lifetime of waitressing in hamburger joints. She practiced Psycho-Imagery for two weeks. Now she's a raving beauty in a bikini on the sands of Miami beaches. What happened? Simply but miraculously, she won a sweepstakes for $540,000!

Leonard T., of Baton Rouge, Louisiana, believed that as a man nearing 50 years of age and confined to a wheelchair, he would never know happiness in this life. After 20 days of practicing Psycho-Image Materialization, a warm-hearted, luscious, young blonde nurse, only 25 years old, fell in love with him, married him, and turned his life into a series of electric days and nights.

Miracles? You bet! *Modern* miracles. And they will happen in your life, too, if you practice the techniques provided for you in this book. Everything you need to turn dismal living into vivacious, dynamic LIFE MORE ABUNDANT is at your beck and call.

Remember this: You are being victimized by outdated, archaic ideas handed down to you by well-meaning people like so many old clothes. You don't have to wear them! Right now you can start thinking for yourself. How do you think for yourself? By erasing old "tapes" in your subconscious mind about what you think you are and who you think other people are. Replace these old, defeating tapes with new ones, fresh ones, inspiring ones. How? Practice, practice, practice Psycho-Image Materialization!

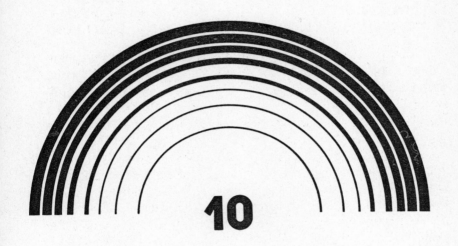

10

How to Control
Thoughts and Feelings
With New Miracle Dynamics

How would you like to affect the thinking of other people so that they *must* help you?

How would you like to attract the opposite sex invisibly and make them need you hungrily?

How would you like to influence your employer's decisions in your favor?

How would you like to attract people with money into your life?

Men and women all over America are now doing these marvelous things, and you can, too. With the help of Psycho-Image Materialization practices, you can manipulate the thoughts and feelings of others so that they *want* to make you happy!

Unbelievable? "If thou canst believe, all things are possible." Once you begin using your Psycho-Imagery, as this chapter teaches, you will not only believe, you will *know*!

Why the Image-Forming Part of Your Mind Will Work Like Magic for You

A smattering of metaphysical insight will help you to understand why your Psycho-Imagery will perform miracles in your life. The part of your mind that forms images is called many things; here, I will use the term "subconscious." Only the subconscious uses images. The conscious mind uses only words and descriptions. And that's a huge difference! The magical, miracle-working portion of your total psyche resides in your subconscious. Now here's the secret to why your Psycho-Imagery will influence the thoughts and feelings of others: there is only *one* subconscious Mind, while there are millions of conscious minds. Put another way, there is only one Higher Self, which we all share in common, while there are millions of small egos. All people are tapped into the same subconscious or Universal Mind—whether they know it or not. If you *know* it, you can use this knowledge for your own benefit. How? By communicating with It through Psycho-Imagery. For more detailed information on this subject I strongly recommend that you read my earlier book, *Helping Yourself with Psychosymbology*.[1]

The point is this: With Psycho-Image Materialization practices, you achieve direct contact with the subconscious Mind of everyone! Therefore you can consciously affect and influence their inner thoughts and feelings so that they will think well of you and feel good about you. Just imagine the infinite possibilities open to you once you perfect this technique for communicating with Universal Mind!

How Psycho-Image Materialization Gives You the Edge in All Human Affairs

Psycho-Image Materialization breaks through the barrier of privacy that separates you from the thoughts and feelings of others. It gives you the secret power to influence, even *command*, others by penetrating their private thoughts!

Every day, people you come into contact with are using the subconscious Mind that embraces all of us. If you tap that common Source of information, you will know what others are thinking and feeling.

You have probably done this a few times in your life already, but in an undisciplined way. You were tapping into Universal Mind when . . .

- A stranger gazed steadily at you for no apparent reason.
- You felt uncomfortable in the presence of another person and had a nagging suspicion there was something "wrong."
- A perfect stranger smiled at you or did something nice for you or felt warm toward you.

---

[1]Theodor Laurence, *Helping Yourself With Psychosymbology*. (West Nyack, New York: Parker Publishing Company, 1978).

There are many instances of this secret contact, too numerous to list. These suffice to show you that every day, all day long, actually, you are in contact with the minds and feelings of others—if you but knew it!

When you discipline this power through your use of Psycho-Image Materialization, you will discover that you possess Mental Vision. With it, you will "see" the thoughts of others and influence them for your own good. With your knowledge of Psycho-Image Materialization you will be able to "tune in" to others any time you wish, learn their secret thoughts and desires, find out how they really feel about you, ascertain the best move to make in their presence so you come out ahead.

How a Successful and Wealthy Poker Player Developed His "Psychic Radar" Through Psycho-Image Materialization

Phil M., of Toledo, Ohio, moved to California six months ago and couldn't find work. With the little money he had, he started playing steady poker in Gardena. He used Psycho-Imagery to become a fantastic winner at the tables. He explained:

> "You have to want to win. You have to really *want* lots of money—almost desperately. Then you have to *concentrate* your images on the channel you want the money to come through. In my case it's poker. A lady friend of mine is an artist. She uses images of people buying her paintings. She rented a storefront and set up her work, and as people came in, she 'tuned in' to their subconscious and showed them exactly what they should buy. She walked away that day with over $5,000. I've learned to tune in to the thoughts and feelings of poker players, and I come out ahead!"

Phil says he spends half an hour each evening practicing affirmations and mind activators. Then he Psycho-Images people around a poker table and always sees himself as winning. He shared one example of how his Psycho-Image Materialization works for him:

> "I was in a game the other night with a guy who bluffed everyone out but me. The man on my right folded. The lady to my left dropped out. This guy kept raising the ante, scaring everybody out of the game. Do you know why they dropped out? Because their systems are based on odds, on counting cards, stuff like that. I don't use those old methods. Not since I learned how to use Psycho-Image Materialization to read minds. I sat there using what I call my Psychic Radar. I just *knew* this guy was bluffing. So I stayed in and I stayed in until he and I were the only ones in. I called the last raise and he showed his hand. Sure enough, he had three aces, all right—but not good enough. I had a straight! I cleaned up about 2,000 bucks that night!"

You can develop your own Psychic Radar the same way Phil did. All it takes is a sincere desire to have money—or love or position or rank or status or whatever you wish in this life! Here's the system Phil used.

Psycho-Image Materialization Affirmation #10

My conscious mind is in tune with the subconscious Mind of all people, near and far. I open to subconscious influx and therefore live in the great reservoir of combined knowledge. I possess the power to assimilate instantly the thoughts and feelings of others. I cannot want for any good thing because my mind is attuned to this subconscious Source of all good. People who will help me are drawn into my sphere.

Each and every day I am enriched by countless

blessings that come to me through others. Money gravitates to me because I command it be so through the subconscious of others. Wealth is mine because people cannot help but enrich me when I contact their subconscious Mind.

I am grateful now for my Psychic Radar with which I see into the secret thoughts of others. I am grateful for my inner hearing with which I detect and differentiate the false and the true. I am grateful for all the wonderful things about to transpire in my life as I contact and tap Universal Mind.

Men and women are even now coming to help me, enrich me, uplift me, encourage me, and sponsor me, for which I am grateful. I now open my mind to Mind, the Source of all good.

Change the Thoughts and Feelings of Others, and You Can't Lose

Practice the above Affirmation diligently until you *feel* yourself at-one with Universal Mind. And know that that Mind is in and through everyone, regardless of appearances or ego-assumptions. It is not what people say or believe that is important to you, but what they ultimately *are*. They are extensions of the same Mind you are. Knowing this, you can consciously develop a power of penetration, as if you had X-ray eyes to see into the secrets of others. But first you must prepare the soil of your mind. That's what all the Affirmations in this potent book are for—to help you till the soil of your miracle-working mind.

Once you have practiced the above Affirmation, you are ready to utilize what it does for you. You can begin to alter the thoughts and feelings of those around you to draw to yourself every good thing you can wish for or think of.

Get alone with yourself. Relax. Be comfortable. And read, read, read the above Affirmation until it becomes a part of you. Then you will be ready to begin a magnificent six-step program to dream-realization.

New Miracle Dynamics Mind Activator #10

Write down and contemplate these six life-changing steps:

1. The Target.
2. The Gratitude.
3. The Psycho-Image.
4. The Enhancement.
5. The Action.
6. The Anticipation.

I. *Choose Your Target Carefully*

Many people wish their lives away. A wish is valueless until you learn how to have it fulfilled. Think: Who can help you attain your goal in life right now? Your mate? Your boss? A millionaire? Pick a target for your subconscious work. Begin by using your Psycho-Imagery ability to focus on a person who can better your life, such as:

- A beautiful woman.
- A rich man.
- A guardian angel.
- A philanthropist.
- A contest judge.

You can even use a photograph of someone you've seen in a magazine or newspaper, as long as it represents someone in a position to help you. See this helpful person in your mind's eye. Relax with the image in your mind. Close your eyes and visualize the person already helping you. Watch in your mind's eye the person come to you and give you precisely what you want.

Imagine the person as having helped you already. Enjoy the feeling of having attained your desire. Open your mind to the truth of it. *Know* that your wish has been granted.

II. *Be Thankful Before You See It with Your Eyes*

Gratitude prior to receipt works miracles! You have a target. You are in touch with it in Mind. Now you must be thankful for what that person is going to do for you—before he or she does it.

What is actually happening is that your Psycho-Imagery is focusing all your latent subconscious power on someone who can make your life better, happier, more fulfilled. That person is automatically, simultaneously being prepared to come to your aid, whether he knows you or not. With no physical effort on your part, with no "convincing" argument for an ego, with no explanation whatsoever about your intentions or needs, you are attracting the help you desire—out of thin air, so to speak.

Remember, miracles do not occur without gratitude prior to receipt.

III. *Psycho-Image Your Way Right into the Heart and Mind of Your Target*

If you have failed continuously at "getting across" to people with words, gestures, pleas, arguments, discussions, and so on, it is time you benefited from the use of Psycho-Imagery. Through this wonder-working mind power, you will penetrate to the very heart and mind of people. Men and women may have set up strong defenses against rational argument and reasonable discussion, but they cannot erect barriers against thought!

Your target is etched in your imagination.

Gratitude prior to receipt has empowered your desire or wish.

Now you are ready to Psycho-Image. Picture it. Imagine the person who can fulfill your wildest dream. *See* him or her arriving to fulfill it. Hear his or her actually knocking on your door. Visualize yourself answering the door, letting the person in, serving coffee, perhaps. Let an entire drama unfold with you and the person as the only actors in it. Whatever your dream or wish is, watch the person bring it to pass. And *thank* him or her!

IV. *How to Enhance the Power of Your Psycho-Imagery for Maximum Results*

There is a trick to making Psycho-Images manifest concretely in your life. Here it is, revealed for your benefit:

1. You enhance your Psycho-Imaging power by thwarting negative ego selfishness in others. Simply say: "No matter what this person's ego thinks, he (or she) *must* help me, and I am grateful."

2. Strengthen your subconscious power by making a thrilling list of all your needs and desires. Write down a Psycho-Image drama for each—and see yourself receiving all you desire.

3. Consciously reinforce your Psycho-Imagery sessions by saying in faith: "My Psycho-Images permeate the atmosphere and travel through space at the speed of light, magnetizing others to come to my aid."

V. *How to Switch From Physical Energy Output to Psychic Energy Output*

Action is your next step to dream-realization through Psycho-Image Materialization. What action? Physical action? Put your nose to the grindstone and your shoulder to the wheel? Get out there and work?

Those are old ideas, and until you let go of them the result is nil. No effort, work or physical energy is required for you to employ the miracle-working power of Psycho-Image Materialization. In fact, these outdated means to wish-fulfillment may even get in your way. Let them go. Psycho-Imaging is the new, dynamic way. It puts at your disposal vast amounts of psychic energy, the energy that transfers at all times between minds, right in the air, like radio and television signals.

Your action consists in closing your eyes, creating sharp, moving pictures of wish-fulfillment, and simply waiting for your dreams to come true.

VI. *Why Expectation and Anticipation Are as Vital as Your Psycho-Images*

Expectation and anticipation are to your Psycho-Images as your heart and brain are to your body. Without your heart and brain you would not function. Similarly, without expectation and anticipation, Psycho-Image Materialization will not function.

To revert to my original example of Jesus and Lazarus, just imagine what·would have happened if, after he prayed, Jesus said, "Well, I've prayed to the Father to raise Lazarus, so my work is finished." Absurd! He went forth *believing*! That's what your expectation and anticipation mean—your belief, your faith.

Anticipate the actualization of your desire. Expect miracles to happen in your life through the people you have been Psycho-Imaging.

Each time a desire is met, create a new one and do these steps over again with the new need or wish. The rest of your life will be one long journey from joy to joy.

How Timothy C. Was Subconsciously Helped to Attract the Sum of $40,000 Through Psycho-Image Materialization

Timothy C. had just been evicted from his apartment for non-payment of past-due rent, and he was sleeping on his brother-in-law's living room sofa. He didn't mind this situation as long as he was able to pay his own way. But the company he worked for laid off over a hundred employees, and Tim was one of them. His sister and brother-in-law assured him he could live with them until he got on his feet but, as far as Tim was concerned, this was an intolerable situation. He went into a deep depression, anxious and worried.

Tim was more than ready for Psycho-Image Materialization, and it saved his life. The moment he discovered the wonder-working principles of this system, he put them into action.

He began by meditating on the six-step program for changing one's luck and life. He knew he couldn't wish his job back or wish for money in the bank. He was thirty years old and had already learned that wishing is for children. What he needed was a hard-line, practical approach to his problems. So he started practicing Psycho-Image Materialization with verve and enthusiasm.

At first he thought he might Psycho-Image his old boss in order to get his former position back in the company. He talked to me about that. I wouldn't discourage a person from using this technique in any way he saw fit, but I couldn't resist pointing out a very important fact: *You can use Psycho-Image Materialization to get ANYTHING you want!*

"Tim," I said, "why be satisfied with crumbs when you can have the whole loaf? Sure, you can use Psycho-Image Materialization to get your job back. But then what? Use it again to get a raise? And again to get a car, a home, clothes, and so on? Why not go whole hog and get the job done once and for all?"

Tim got my point and returned home to get busy. He told me later how he used Psycho-Image Materialization. He showed up in my temporary headquarters with a gorgeous woman on his arm, and they'd arrived in a brand new Cadillac! He was the vice-president of a large corporation, drawing a salary of $75,000.00 a year! How did all this happen?

Grinning from ear to ear, he sat across from my desk in a $200 suit and said, "When I did step one of your program, I made a target of every person you mentioned: a beautiful woman, a rich man, a guardian angel, a philanthropist, and a contest judge! I used pictures of each of them."

He went on to explain that he began with a photo of a luscious, beautiful woman from a popular magazine. He relaxed with the image of the woman in his mind. He "saw" her come to him in the night and express tremendous love and passion for him.

Then he used a picture of the millionaire, J. Paul Getty, to help him attain riches. For a guardian angel, he employed the photograph of a classic painting of an angel in his Bible.

"I don't know any philanthropists or contest judges," he said, "so I just used pictures that seemed right for the purpose."

Two weeks later things began to happen in Tim's life. Amazing things. Remarkable things. Right from the start, miracles occurred. He received a call from his old employer (whom he was not using in his Psycho-Image Materialization exercises) and the man asked him to come back to work. Tim declined the offer. He'd decided to commit himself to Psycho-Image work. And it paid off.

He thanked each Psycho-Image for already helping him. He visualized himself getting all the wonderful things he wanted in life. He enhanced his Psycho-Imagery by writing down everything he wanted. He "saw" in his mind's eye every single wish coming true. Then he waited with expectation and anticipation.

"Here's the amazing thing!" Tim exclaimed. "When I was working for peanuts in that other company, they ran a little contest for the employees to see if they could come up with some money-saving ideas. I entered the contest, but my idea was a loser. That's what I was told. They threw my diagrams away. Or thought they did. Some secretary must have gotten them mixed up in official papers. I had been practicing

Psycho-Image Materialization, oh, maybe ten days, when I got this call from a Mr. Terrence L. What my old company didn't like, this man raved about! He said he could see a lot of work went into the idea and he wanted to meet me. He thought I was working for the old outfit and he asked me if he could tempt me away from it with a fat salary. I told him honestly that I was no longer with that firm, and he was delighted! I said I was certainly interested in working for him, and he said he'd send a car for me in the morning.

"Guess who was driving that car? Yep, this lovely lady right here, Sheila. Mr. L. sent his own private secretary to pick me up! And am I glad he did!"

Sheila broke in to share Tim's pleasure in all this, because, as she put it, she "fell head over heels" for him immediately.

"I got everything I Psycho-Imaged!" Tim laughed heartily. "Sheila's not only my lover, she's my secretary! I wasn't in the firm a week when Mr. L. simply raised me to the level of vice-president!"

"The Caddy? Heck, I entered some silly contest that came in the mail. I used to call it junk mail. Some outfit was selling some kind of a product by mail, and the instructions said I could order or not order by choice, but either way I could enter their contest. So I did. I won first prize!"

Tim grew more and more excited as he rattled off all the things Psycho-Image Materialization did for him, until both he and Sheila were like two laughing, happy children. I couldn't help chuckling myself, because their joy was contagious.

"I'm making $75,000.00 a year now! But that isn't the half of it! You know that contest I mentioned? I didn't win only a Cadillac. I got a cash award of exactly the amount I was Psycho-Imaging—$40,000!"

If Tim were any happier that day, they would have had to come and take him away!

You, Too, Can Manifest Your Desires Quickly and Easily

Study this chapter as thoroughly and vigorously as all the others and you, too, will share in the kind of joy Tim experiences today.

Make a comprehensive list of all the things you want out of life. Then practice, practice, practice your Psycho-Image Materialization program as outlined for you. Check off each miracle as it occurs in your life, always remembering to be *grateful prior to receipt!*

In time you will be delighted to see that your Psycho-Image Materialization practices pay off! You will be amazed when total strangers become life-long friends and sponsors, helping you toward higher goals and richer living. You will be astounded how Psycho-Image Materialization influences and affects the thoughts and feelings of others so that you come out ahead.

One day Tim did not know Sheila or Mr. L. The next day Sheila was his sweetheart and Mr. L. his appreciative employer! Just like that! Latch on to this miracle-working power yourself—right now! And enjoy!

11

The Secret of Forever Banishing Fears, Doubts, Setbacks, and Obstacles

There is a world of joy, fun, and fulfillment at your fingertips. Why should fear and doubt rob you of your birthright? You *deserve* the good things in life. You were *meant* to enjoy them. If you are not—why not? What blocks you from enjoying life more abundant?

Perhaps you have no idea. I hear from hundreds of men and women from all walks of life who do not know what obstacles keep them from enjoying a fuller, richer life.

Guess what? You don't *have* to know! This is the amazing message from Psycho-Image Materialization. All you need is a strong desire to be fulfilled here and now, as well as some secrets to the powerful use of your mind and imagination.

This chapter will guide you in your use of Psycho-Image Materialization to render impotent any unknown or unseen force that keeps you from living anything but a perfect life. You will be amazed to see how obstacles and setbacks— whether people, places or things—disappear like magic when you use Psycho-Image Materialization exercises.

The Psycho-Image Materialization Secret to Inner and Outer Balance

Many of the men and women who write to me seem to suffer the inability to make inner wishes and dreams outer realities. You need not suffer this basic and seemingly irreconcilable dichotomy of nature. Psycho-Image Materialization makes the two ONE! That's its purpose—to give you the means to realizing your hopes and dreams. In this sense, Psycho-Image Materialization is your *bridge* that spans the chasm between inner and outer, a way to achieve and enjoy the better things in this life here and now.

How does Psycho-Image Materialization accomplish this immense task? It does so because it is based upon the ancient but ever potent truth that all is Mind, that in reality there is no difference between *your* mind and *the* Mind. Indeed,

Psycho-Image Materialization teaches that your mind is a *channel* for Mind. When you learn how to channel Mind, nothing can be denied you! This is precisely how Edgar Cayce was able to perform the remarkable mind-power feats he did: his mind was in perfect tune with Universal Mind. Hence, he could "read" the minds of all people, no matter where they were. When you are in tune with Mind, time and space lose all meaning. There is only here and now. Through Psycho-Image Materialization, you will learn how to "read" whatever you wish here and now. You will be using Mind-stuff— ectoplasmic essence—and you will be able to mold it, shape it, rework it. In this way you will be able to annihilate fears and doubts, setbacks, and obstacles to your good fortune and happiness. For all these negatives are merely the misuse of Mind-stuff by others. And you can change it!

To use this vast supply of power, it is necessary to be *receptive* to it. Your mind has to be open to Universal Mind. Psycho-Image Materialization is your key to the prerequisite opening. Many people do not know how to open to this miraculous force. Some don't even know it exists. For these people, life is a long series of accidents and chances, fate, and question. They are bound by fears, doubts, setbacks, and obstacles.

When you practice the principles of Psycho-Image Materialization, *you* make the decisions about what you want out of life. *Nothing* can stand in your way. But before you can remove obstacles, you must recognize that there are some.

Make a List of the People, Places, and Things Blocking You from Perfect Happiness

Remember that through Psycho-Image Materialization, you can reach into the minds of others and influence them. You can use the same method to annihilate fears and doubts. Setbacks and obstacles will fall away as your mind becomes attuned to Universal Mind.

Are you afraid of something? Do doubts nag you and keep you from life more abundant? Do conditions and circumstances block your way to successful living? Are there people in your way? Make a list of all these things. Remember: it is not negative to study negative things. It is a creative act to look closely at what hampers you, binds you, keeps you down. Then you can deal with it.

If you desired to take a trip but have no car, the negative "no car" has to be dealt with first. The trip is yours already, but you have to come up with transportation. So it is with the good things of life. They are already yours. All you have to do is get rid of the negatives standing between you and perfect living. You do that with Psycho-Image Materialization.

Let's say that you wish to have $100,000.00 in the bank. The question is not, "Why don't I have it?" The question is, "What is keeping me from it?" Find out what is keeping you from receiving all that you desire, make a list, and then start using Psycho-Image Materialization to banish the obstacles. Don't let yourself be held back by people, places, and things. You now possess the key to life fulfillment.

Pause Each Day to Show Gratitude Prior to Receipt

Do not focus on things you do not have. Focus on all the riches and beauty that are yours for the asking! Be thankful for the wealth and treasures available to you right now. Know what you want and be thankful for it before you even see it!

I begin each day with an attitude of gratitude. I arise and thank God for this very day. Just to wake up is a miracle, you know. Some people don't! So I awaken and express gratitude that I can function and live yet another wondrous day on this beautiful earth. This alone gives me a good feeling, and this feeling accompanies me throughout the day, no matter what happens. This feeling, this attitude, is my key to successful living—each and every day. I do not permit *appearances* to fool me or depress me or exert negative forces on me. I go forth *knowing* that my Psycho-Image Materialization exercises are working—sight unseen. Then they manifest in marvelous ways!

The attitude of gratitude keeps the communication lines

open between my mind and Universal Mind. Universal Mind likes to be *thanked*. But it must be *unconditional* gratitude, that is, you don't thank God because He did something for you or because He will do something for you or if He will do something for you—you simply thank Him for being there at all! Then "all these things will be added unto you."

Once you establish open communication with Universal Mind it will never cease so long as you continue to practice Psycho-Image Materialization.

How to Get Exactly What You Want in Life Regardless of Adverse Conditions

The best way to deal with fears, doubts, setbacks, and obstacles is to be aware of them first. Become familiar with the conditions or circumstances that block your desires. Once you identify the particular negative that is interfering with your complete happiness, you can nullify it with the Psycho-Image Materialization exercise in this chapter.

How a 16-Year-Old Girl Saved Her Brother's Life in a Miraculous Manner

There is more to your practice of Psycho-Image Materialization than meets the eye! A case in point is that of Debbie R., of San Antonio, Texas. She had been using these exercises and programs to make her life happier. She used Psycho-Image Materialization to get herself a TV for her own room, new dresses, money for movies and ice cream, and so on. (See Chapter 12: "Psycho-Image Materialization for Fun and Profit.)

The more you use the system outlined in this book, the more attuned you become to higher-than-human power. Debbie learned this truth in a dramatic way.

One afternoon her brother Tom was working under his car in the back yard. It had rained the night before. The ground was soft and mushy. Though he used a wooden block under the jack, the jack slipped. Debbie heard her brother's horrifying scream. She dashed to the back door and looked out. She almost fainted at what she saw.

Tom was pinned beneath his car, his face distorted in a mask of agony, his eyes bulging in his head. The weight was directly on his chest—and increasing by the second.

In a split second, Debbie evaluated the situation. No help was near. It was up to her. What could she do to save her brother? It looked like the front end of the car was about to crush his rib cage.

Debbie saw the "obstacle" to her effectiveness: strength. Immediately—almost automatically because she'd been practicing Psycho-Image Materialization for months—she "pictured" herself able to lift that car from her brother's body.

Her legs carried her to the car and without a thought of impossibility, she bent down, gripped the bumper, and lifted the car up into the air as if it were made of papier mâché!

This incident made all the headlines, and no wonder! A 16-year-old girl who hadn't lifted anything heavier than school books for most of her young life was able to lift a 3,000-pound automobile! In her Psycho-Image—charged with a desperate desire to help—she "saw" herself lifting the car easily. And she did!

The obstacle—"no strength"—was combatted immediately with a strong Psycho-Image that overcame it. This is an astounding story. But here's something even more astounding: What Debbie did, you can do!

Let a car *symbolize* anything that blocks your success. Name it—fear, doubt, enemy, lack of finances, little opportunity, etc. Now "see" yourself lifting the car easily and effortlessly. You will achieve your goal just as Debbie did! PICTURE IT!

How Richard M. Progressed from a Penniless Cab Driver to a Man Worth Over $500,000

Richard M., of Toledo, Ohio, didn't have a pot or a window, as the saying goes. And he was miserable. He was a cabdriver, working over 60 hours a week for little pay. He was overworked and underpaid. But that isn't the only reason he felt miserable. He thought Fate was against him. It seemed like everyone else was getting all the good breaks in life while he had to suffer a meager existence.

One of his brothers, not as intelligent as Richard, invested in a land deal. It cost the man his savings of $2,000, and Richard thought he was stupid. Richard scoffed, "I wouldn't touch a deal like that with a ten-foot pole!" But his brother went ahead. Six months later a large corporation bought the property and Richard's brother realized a profit *six times* greater than his investment! Richard went into a depression.

An old school buddy wrote to Richard and told him he had just quit his slave-labor job and bought into a department store—a ground floor opportunity. This news further depressed Richard and made him envious of his friend. "Why can't I get breaks like that?" he cried.

His depression deepened, and a feeling of abject hopelessness overcame him to such an extent that even his cabdriving job was in jeopardy. Richard was "doing himself in," and he knew it. In desperation, he called another friend and asked what he could do before he went down the tubes entirely. His friend recommended him to me. That's how I met Richard, a worried, defeated man loaded with resentments, angers, and jealousies.

Right from the start, I told Richard that his enemy was not "bad breaks" or "lack of opportunity." His enemy was "attitude." He needed a newer, fresher outlook on things, and Psycho-Image Materialization could help him. I gave him the techniques that follow so he could banish the fears and doubts blocking his way to a fuller, richer life.

Richard used the mini-program for ten days. Then he called me and was in such a state of excited agitation I could hardly understand what he was telling me. But I got the gist of it. The owner of the taxi company for whom Richard worked had suffered a massive heart attack. Through his attorney he asked Richard to please, *please* manage the company until he could come back to it. Richard plunged right into the task, glad to be out of the cab. For this alone he was grateful, but he continued to practice gratitude prior to receipt.

His boss's heart condition worsened and the doctor's advice was that he retire—right now! Well, the man tried. He stayed home and attempted to rest, but he'd always been an active man, and he wouldn't stick to his resolve. One day, after just a few days at home, he keeled over from exertion. In short, he dropped dead.

Richard feared for his job the minute he heard the dreadful news, but now he had Psycho-Image Materialization to help him through the negative time. He kept "picturing" himself as successful and rich.

Ten days after I met him, he received word that his boss, out of *gratitude*, had willed the company to him! Almost overnight, Richard went from poverty and resentment to riches and happiness. Today he is the sole owner of his own cab company, raking in thousands of dollars. Right now he's worth well over $500,000!

The icing on the cake, as far as Richard is concerned, was two letters, one from his brother and one from his old buddy. Both wanted to know how in heck he got so lucky!

The Psycho-Image Materialization Technique that Makes You a Conqueror and a Winner

This chapter contains the technique that Richard and Debbie have been using constantly. It is presented here just for you. It is time for you to "get the breaks," the opportunities, the chances at fuller, richer living. Many hundreds of men and women are using this technique daily, and they are accruing money, love, friendship, glory, fame, popularity, and hundreds of other good things of life. You will, too.

As always with Psycho-Image Materialization, your mind has to be prepared. You begin with an attitude of open acceptance, of gratitude, of thankfulness for all the wonderful things you desire but do not yet see with your eyes. All the happy, successful people I know begin with this basic tenet—gratitude prior to receipt. Then they practice this:

Psycho-Image Materialization Affirmation #11

Knowing that all my outer conditions begin in my mind, I rid my thoughts of all negativity. All fears, doubts, setbacks, and obstacles to my complete happiness are now dispersing like fog in a strong wind.

Nothing can be denied me as I sit in stillness of Mind, free of darkness and dread. I wish all good for everyone, including myself. I do not envy others their good fortune, but patiently await my own. Great wealth and sustained happiness are coming to me even as I mouth these words.

My mind is attuned to Universal Mind; therefore, only health, wealth, success, and happiness can come to me. As a channel for Infinite Intelligence I can be deterred from my goals by no obstacle; no setback can long keep me from my desires; no darkness, no evil, no negativity can possibly interfere with the power of my Psycho-Images.

As I use Psycho-Imagery to express my needs and desires, I know that outer conditions will re-form themselves to my good.

I am success and happiness. There is no more joy and fulfillment within anyone else than there is in me. I am not my body but a state of mind. I banish every negative person, place, and thing from my life, my thoughts, my feelings. I am free, free, free! I let go of other things and other people, I go forward now in confidence, might, and power, and I conquer all that would block my happiness and success.

> *I release everyone and everything in the world to grow as it must, and in this way I assure my own growth and development. I am receiving love, health, wealth, and happiness, and I am grateful now.*

You Have Just Done Yourself the Biggest Favor in Your Life

Now you have prepared your mind for the influx of Universal Mind. The preceding Psycho-Image Materialization Affirmation is designed to help you open to this influx. When you recite—mentally or orally—this Affirmation, you are doing what gardeners do to soil, what sculptors do to clay: You are remolding Mind-stuff in preparation for the final creation—the realization of your dreams.

Repeat the Affirmation at least once a day for a few days. Let it act as a yeast in your subconscious mind. In fact, let it replace thoughts of worry, dread, or concern. Let this Affirmation begin your day.

Once your mind is attuned to Universal Mind through the daily use of the Affirmation, you are ready to go into action with the following 12-step program.

New Miracle Dynamics Mind Activator #11

This program will help you achieve your life's goals—*in spite of setbacks and obstacles!* It is a paradoxical program.

What is a paradox? A paradox is a statement that appears to be false but is actually true. For example: "I die that I might live"; "I suffer that I may be healed"; "I surrender to become the victor."

Your *New Miracle Dynamics Mind Activator*

#11 is such a paradox based not on worldly teachings, but on metaphysical truths. It will teach you the great worth of surrender to Universal Mind. Until the almighty ego surrenders to this higher power, the higher power cannot work in your life. This is the meaning of humility, meekness, poorness in spirit, and "letting go and letting God."

Read the 12 steps through, get acquainted with them, and then start practicing them. Some people I know take one step at a time. They meditate upon it first thing in the morning and let it manifest in their life before going on to the next step. In the beginning, however, you should thoroughly acquaint yourself with the *feeling of surrender* underlying the program. Here are the 12 wonder-working steps for you.

Step 1: Say to yourself mentally or orally:

I give up! Grunting and groaning simply does not work. As hard as I wish for things, they don't manifest. So I now turn my will and my life over to a power greater than myself, a power that can manifest the things I want in life. I surrender to Universal Mind this day and let It guide my total life.

Step 2: Make this your daily creed:

I believe that Universal Mind can do for me what I cannot do for myself. I believe that as I surrender to this greater power, all good comes to me automatically and effortlessly. I willingly get myself out of the way and permit Universal Mind to take over my life and its affairs.

Step 3: Make this your daily decision:

As tempted as I may be at times, I will not take back my promise to let Universal Mind guide my affairs. I have made my decision to let It rule my life and I will not go back on my word. As I sit in perfect serenity, higher powers work for me. This is my confidence!

Step 4: Make this your periodic practice:

Every once in a while I will make a list of the people, places, and things that seem to interfere with my total happiness. I will list wrongs, injustices, hatreds, and fears. And then I will turn the whole list over to Universal Mind and never act upon it myself. I am nestled in the loving hands of a power greater than myself.

Step 5: Make this your daily admission:

I admit that I have been trained to go about living in the wrong way, trying to change the outer instead of the inner, depending on outside influences and changes instead of inner guidance and direction. The world teaches me to work hard and to get what I want through blood, sweat, and tears. I thoroughly reject this premise today. A higher power will work for me to the degree that I let go of power fantasies. God has all power; I have none. If any fellow human being asks me why things go so well in my life, I will gladly share the knowledge of Psycho-Image Materialization with him.

Step 6: Make this your daily assertion:

I will let Universal Mind remove all setbacks and obstacles to my happiness—even when such setbacks and obstacles are self-made. I do not want anything to stand between me and the realization of my hopes and dreams. Therefore, I let go absolutely and turn the burden over to my higher power— Universal Mind.

Step 7: Make this your daily prayer:

O Universal Mind (or *"Dear God,"* if you wish), *help me to get out of the way of Your movement in my life. Help me to overcome ego direction and to surrender to Your higher will. Remove from my path all that blocks me from total and perfect living. I surrender to Your will with gratitude, knowing beyond doubt that You and You alone can make straight my path, free of obstacles. Remove the source and cause of all my fears and doubts, even those I do not recognize. My life is in Your hands.*

Step 8: Make this your vow for life:

If in my quest for health, wealth, and success I have hurt any fellow human being, forgive me now. I will do all I can to make amends for my wrongs and mistakes. When I am healthy, wealthy, successful, and happy, I will find those people who have helped me along the way and help them in return. I am willing to share my phenomenal happiness and success with others.

Step 9: Make this your first act of charity:

If someone from my past has helped me and I find them in financial difficulties, I will share my wealth with them. If someone from my past has helped me and I find them questing for success, I will share my experience, strength, and hope with them. Whenever I can, wherever I can, I will help those who have helped me. Finally, I will always be willing to share the secrets of Psycho-Image Materialization with anyone in dire need of help.

Step 10: Make this your daily regime:

Each and every day I will pause for a few

moments in silence and review my own behavior, needs, and desires. If I find myself exerting my own will in daily matters, I will apologize to Universal Mind for my pride, and I will immediately turn everything back over to It. In short, I will surrender to higher powers every single day.

Step 11: Make this your daily exercise:

I will use Psycho-Imagery to stay in direct contact with Universal Mind, for, through the practice of Psycho-Image Materialization, I am actually turning my will and my life over to God, which is as it should be.

Step 12: Make this your daily promise:

Having achieved health, wealth, success and happiness as a result of practicing Psycho-Image Materialization, I will try to share my joy with others and continue to practice my techniques in every area of my life. I will not turn some things over and keep some. I will turn my whole life on a daily basis over to Universal Mind and let higher forces operate freely in me, through me, as me, and for me. I so promise!

Through New Miracle Dynamics, You Become a Partner in the Creation of Your New Life

Now you have it. Through your practice of the above Affirmation and 12 Steps, you are in actuality making yourself an active partner in the creation of a whole new life. Don't miss this chance! *Use* your 12-step program as if your life depended on it. You and Universal Mind are now partners, and, because of this fact, all good things will come to you. The operative phrases are: "If God be for me, who can be against me?" and "With God, all things are possible." This chapter will help you to *realize* the truth in these statements. As Emerson put it: "A man is what he thinks all day long." And Aurelius said: "Our life is what our thoughts make it."

"With the help of the dynamic programs in this book, Psycho-Image Materialization will change your thoughts and mind. You will be a veritable *magnet*, attracting to yourself constantly all the wonderful, happy, and delightful things in life. With Psycho-Image Materialization, you can kiss fears, doubts, setbacks, and obstacles goodbye!

Picture It! And go forth conquering!

12

Psycho-Image Materialization
for Fun and Profit

This chapter is designed to help you achieve more fun out of life. So far we have concentrated on the serious problems we all have, and rightly so, for until we solve some of our basic troubles, life is no fun. In what follows, you will learn a new attitude, with the help of the Psycho-Image Materialization Affirmation and the New Miracle Dynamics Mind Activator, an attitude that will bring you a lighter spirit, a healthier outlook on life, and the opportunity to have relaxing, therapeutic *fun*.

Psycho-Image Materialization has solved many of my problems over the years, just as it will yours. But I have also allowed myself the pleasure of gaining fun and pleasure and profit and gain from these potent exercises. Why not? You have suffered enough in this world and you deserve—as well as need—more fun. I discovered a source of pleasure in Psycho-Image Materialization and I *claimed* it, expressing gratitude prior to receipt at all times. As Rudyard Kipling once put it: "I've taken my fun where I've found it."

Expect fun in your life when you begin to practice the steps outlined for you in this chapter. I include this facet of Psycho-Image Materialization for good reason: While you are in the process of bettering and enhancing your life, which is heavy work, you should learn to relax and enjoy each and every day. The goals you have set yourself, your dreams and wishes, these may take time to manifest concretely. While you are waiting, you should not walk about with a long face, fretting about the future. Live one day at a time—and make it fun! Your subconscious will do the rest!

Use each chapter in this book wholeheartedly to achieve the aims of your life. But every once in a while, practice the technique outlined in this chapter. It's like taking a break when climbing Mount Everest, like resting when swimming the English Channel. After all, you are remaking your very life. Though you may be a serious and dedicated student of metaphysics, you are also human. You need rest, relaxation,

fun, and pleasure, too. So, prepare your subconscious for
these things.

Psycho-Image Materialization Affirmation #12

*Mind, as First Cause, is the beginning and
ending of all my fun and pleasure. Universal
Mind provides, nurtures, and sustains all that It
gives so freely. It is the Giver of good things, and
I now claim my share. As I Psycho-Image unlimited fun and pleasure, I gratefully accept my
abundance already winging its way to me, awaiting only my openness.*

*Pleasure, fun, money, excitement—symbols
of my inner acceptance—flow easily into my life.
I observe that in many words, I am daily reminded that Mind is the ONE provider of all my
good: mONEy, hONEy, alONE, thrONE, etc. This
magnanimous Mind, eternally free of finite lim-
itations, is my source of all good. I gratefully
Psycho-Image this source as my Friend, Guide,
Partner, and Supporter, knowing beyond a doubt
and in spite of appearances that It will make my
days and nights peaceful, fulfilling, fun, and
pleasurable. For this I am now thankful.*

Through the Magic of Psycho-Image Materialization, You Attract Fun and Pleasure on Command

How would you like to go on a picnic with a beautiful
woman or a handsome man? *Picture It!*

How about a week off with pay? *Picture It!*

Maybe you would enjoy astral travel or communication
with higher spiritual beings. *Picture It!*

Would you like to take a journey in a UFO and learn from the wisdom of Masters? *Picture It!*

How about earning $150,000.00 more this year than last? *Picture It!*

Universal Mind does not hold back—ever! *Picture It* and *get* it! Universal Mind operates on the principle of Unconditional Love: It provides your wants and needs not *because* you did something for it nor because you *will* do something nor *if* you do something. Mind provides because It loves you just as you are! *It* is your Friend. *Picture It!*

A man once asked me, "How can I get the car my family needs if I don't have any money to buy it?"

"Can you picture yourself in a new car?" I countered.

"Of course," he replied. "I can use Psycho-Imagery the way you say, but what's that got to do with concrete reality?"

I felt like saying, "Oh, ye of little faith!" but I didn't. I think it would not have been compassionate. Instead, I placed a hand on his shoulder, looked into his troubled eyes, and said, "*Picture It* and you've got it."

Within two weeks he was the astounded owner of a brand new Cadillac! How he got it is not really important. What is important is that he ceased doubting the power of Psycho-Imagery and received exactly what he wanted. Oh, it wasn't the car he pictured, nor the color and size—but it was an automobile, exactly as he gave the picture to his subconscious!

A young woman was having trouble winning the love of an important businessman. She kept picturing herself married to him.

"It isn't working," she said.

"Marriage comes *after* courtship and maybe even some fun necking. Have you Psycho-Imaged that?"

"Goodness, no!" she blushed.

"Do it!" I said. "Imagine yourself going to his apartment in a slinky dress, beautiful as the morning sun. See yourself embracing him, pressing against him, arousing him, interesting him, motivating him. No one knows your Psycho-Images. Feel free. Get the guy's motor running, for goodness sake!"

She did, he did, and they did!

Remember That Your Psycho-Images Are Requests and That Universal Mind Never Says No

Do you know why people lead fruitless, dissatisfying lives? They asked for them! Yes, it's quite true. You see, Universal Mind, the power Psycho-Image Materialization puts you in direct touch with, accepts all thoughts, feelings and desires as images-in-the-form-of-requests. And Mind never says no to anything! Here's an example:

A man in Oregon was down in the dumps. He said, "I'm a failure." Without his knowing, his mind translated these words into an image of failure that was then transferred to the subconscious. Universal Mind, which always says Yes, simply said: "Yes, you are a failure." And he was!

Use your imagination creatively with Psycho-Image Materialization exercises! *Picture* yourself winning, loving, having fun, enjoying an exciting, successful life. With Psycho-Image Materialization you will cease transmitting bad images of yourself to your subconscious, and you will be better off for it.

Remember this—write it down if it will help imbed it in your fertile mind: Psycho-Images trigger subconscious response. Subconscious response creates outer experience, your "world." Outer experience makes you happy or sad. That brings us full circle, doesn't it? If your conditions and circumstances are not the best, change it all with Psycho-Image Materialization. *Picture It!* And be thankful prior to receipt of the wonderful, pleasurable things about to happen to you. *Expect* results! Expectation is one of the keys to materialization. Expectation smacks of faith, trust, belief, and gratitude.

How to Have a Great Deal of Fun and Pleasure While Your Life Is Improving Magically

Many people pray for something and then wait with white knuckles and gritted teeth for the answer. Absurd! You are permitted to enjoy this life while you are awaiting its improvement. This book is showing you how to Psycho-Image for your betterment. Chapter after chapter guides you to the realization of life more abundant. The preceding chapters deal with some of the headiest issues known to man. Now it is time to "let go and let God," as it were.

In this fun chapter, the object is to Psycho-Image a short-range goal, The achievement of which will make you happier *today*.

New Miracle Dynamics Mind Activator #12

Picture It:

- You meet and entertain a man or woman who lends zest to your day.
- You move into a new home that delights you.
- You are offered a job that pays three times what you are earning now.
- If you are a student, you now possess the power to pass all exams effortlessly.
- You win a big-money contest or even a small game of Bingo.

The point is to Psycho-Image something that will make you smile or feel pleased. We are unique individuals with different likes and dislikes. Figure out what you would like right now—sex, money, love, power, freedom—whatever it is, it will come to you in a form reserved for you by Universal Mind.

Once you have *Pictured It*, set the book aside for a few moments and contemplate the imagery of having *already* received your reward.

Bathe in the *feeling* of accomplishment.

Notice details of the wonderful event. Psycho-Image it as real.

For example, if your desire is a business of your own, visualize yourself already possessing it, operating it, enjoying it. Have fun Psycho-Imaging your success!

Here's a personal story for readers of this book. Twenty years ago I was in dire circumstances, unfulfilled, unhappy, with seemingly no way out. Certain books—inspirational, uplifting books—helped me through the rough spots. I vowed right then that someday I would write such books. When I started using the techniques outlined here for you, I Psycho-Imaged myself writing books for the company that published the books that helped me so much. That "idle daydream" has come true. In fact, you are reading a product of the reality. I am now writing books to help others!

I relate this story only to point out that I'm not telling you anything here that hasn't already worked in my own life. I am sharing the secrets of Psycho-Image Materialization with you because they worked for me! If they have worked for me, they will work for you! Bank on it!

You are now an experienced Psycho-Image Materializer. You are in direct contact with a loving Universal Mind that can fulfill any Psycho-Image you transmit to It.

Take these steps:

1. Psycho-Image anything you can think of that will make you very happy right now.
2. See yourself in your mind's eye enjoying the fulfillment of this wish.
3. Accept the fact that Universal Mind has only good for you. It is not a moral judge. Anything you want can be yours through this practice.

4. Application is your next step. What should you apply? No, not physical energy. Not work. Not blood, sweat, and tears. Psycho-Image Materialization is your new way of getting things for nothing, so to speak. Through your mental pictures, you avail yourself of wonder-working life energy that can't say no to you! So, apply your mind, your spirit, your emotions, and your wishes, hopes, and desires!

5. Last but not least, *expect*. Right after a Psycho-Image session, end with some kind of softly spoken prayer of gratitude. Then let go and let Universal Mind bring you happiness.

6. Keep it simple and make it fun!

How a Woman's Psycho-Image Helped Her to Read the Mind of the Man She Desired

People keep secrets, and even though the keeping of secrets may make others feel you are standoffish, we all like someone to "see through" us, to help us overcome reluctance and inhibition. Such was the experience of Donna L., a secretary in New York. She longed for the love of a particular man, a Mr. T., but she was profoundly aware that he had "built walls" around himself. He seemed unapproachable.

Donna came to me with her problem: "I love this guy, but I'm not getting to first base with him. What can I do? I mean, he smiles at me when I smile, but he hasn't even asked me out to dinner or anything. I'm so frustrated!"

"Make it fun," I suggested. "The next time you use Psycho-Image Materialization, see him with you. Enjoy his company. Get on the sofa with him. Sit on his lap. Curl your fingers through his hair. Kiss him. Caress him. His subconscious will pick up all these warm feelings, and he'll warm up to you."

Donna gave it a try—and had a most remarkable experience. She explained, "I was in a coffee shop with Mr. T. We met there, so I asked him if I might sit with him. I guess my frustrated desires are making me bold! But he of course offered a chair and I sat down. As we talked idly and sipped coffee, I Psycho-Imaged him as my lover—a real, passionate, caring lover.

"Suddenly a great wave of sadness came over me, almost overwhelmed me. An aura of mystery engulfed the booth that we were sitting in, and I found myself staring down into my cup like a tea-leaf reader. I suddenly "saw" that Mr. T. had a terrible secret burdening him."

Donna couldn't hold her tongue. She looked up at the man and put her hand over his. "It isn't your fault that your wife died in that car accident," she murmured.

Mr. T. almost went into a state of shock. "What? But . . . how . . . how did you know about that? No one knows about my personal life, my grief, my guilt."

"You're not guilty," Donna said softly. "You didn't feel like going to the store with her, that's all. She went alone and didn't blame you. Even when the car crashed into that tree, she held no ill feelings toward you. You've been suffering this guilt much too long."

Needless to say, the secretive man was dazed. Tears welled in his eyes, and Donna's kind and almost sacred words—"You're not guilty"—burned in his ears. For the first time in years he was able to unburden his soul to another human being, a person who cared.

Then the fun began. Donna recalls that once Mr. T. was able to unload his guilt, he became rejuvenated, happy, and electric. It turned out that he had once been a very active man, full of life and a lover of pleasures.

Freed from his burden, he gravitated to Donna like an iron nail to a magnet. Donna reports: "He takes me to such fabulous places now! We went on a scenic cruise in the Caribbean. We laughed and danced in Disneyworld. We dine out almost every evening in sumptuous, glorious clubs. From that day to this, I haven't had another dull moment. I can't believe how much fun I'm having! And I owe it all to Psycho-Image Materialization."

It wouldn't surprise me if Donna wrote soon and mentioned marriage!

How Lisa D. Escaped a Life of Drudgery and Loneliness and Emerged Bright, Happy, and Vivacious

Lisa D., of Scranton, Pennsylvania, was one of the most brow-beaten, lonely, depressed women I have ever known. She'd been married to a drunken sot who was an inveterate wife-beater. He constantly abused Lisa, and for her there was no escape. She was afraid to leave the man because she had no one to turn to. Her parents were dead. No brothers or sisters. She felt hemmed in by Fate. She married in 1975, and finances were low, also making it impossible for her to better herself. The years seemed to drag by. Night after night her husband would come home drunk, surly, and mean. He beat her for no good reason (not that there is *any* reason to strike a woman). Year after year Lisa despaired, and her financial condition grew worse and worse. She was absolutely dependent upon this man who hated her and abused her.

But then came her discovery of Psycho-Image Materialization. Just when things seemed darkest, this wonder-working power came to her aid. She wanted freedom, lightness, gaiety, laughter, some fun in life. And she got it all! Here is what she reports:

"I've always liked the Cinderella fairy tale, so I used it as a Psycho-Image, with me as Cinderella. In faith and trust I practiced Psycho-Image Materialization daily, seeing a Prince Charming coming to rescue me, a man who would kiss me tenderly, embrace me lovingly, hold me tight as if he couldn't live without me. I've always wanted that.

"But that isn't what I got. I got more than that from Psycho-Image Materialization! My husband was drunk one day when he beat me and stalked out of the house, never to return. To this day I don't

know what happened to him or where he is. Now I
don't care where he is!

"At first I was frightened and alone. Then I used
Psycho-Image Materialization to get myself a job.
Not just *any* job. Now that I was free of that ty-
rant, I wanted fun! So I pictured myself as a
stewardess.

"Today I *am* a stewardess! I own my own spiffy
roadster. I have two apartments, one in Florida and
one in San Francisco. As for kisses, embraces, and
love—well, I'll just say that I have an address book
that would make Farrah Fawcett's eyes turn green
with envy!"

Use Your New Psycho-Imagery Power to Brighten Your Life

You are invited to share in the fun and pleasure being
enjoyed today by thousands of men and women from all walks
of life. Use Psycho-Image Materialization techniques to enhance your love life, increase your fun, multiply your pleasures. Life is to be lived, not worried over! Mind is a mystery
to be enjoyed, not a problem to be solved. Use Mind, and
Mind will bless you!

I took a poll recently, the results of which I would like to
share with you. I wrote to several men and women and point-
edly asked them in a questionnaire how they used Psycho-
Image Materialization for fun. Here are some of the replies I
received:

- Jane Y., of Cheyenne, Wyoming, reports that she
  Psycho-Imaged herself winning a big sweepstakes.
  She says:

  > "I asked my Higher Power for the name
  > of the winning horse. At that very mo-
  > ment a great rush of wind howled outside
  > my house. I didn't get the connection until
  > I looked in the paper and saw the name of
  > a horse: Howling Wind. A rush of excite-

ment convinced me, and I bet on the horse. The race and the sweepstakes were held in New Jersey. I won! Since then I use Psycho-Image Materialization for fun in Las Vegas and Reno. My winnings so far amount to $240,000.00!"

- Kirk M., of Albuquerque, New Mexico, dropped out of school when he was a child. Since then, he has labored as a car mechanic, working and slaving to make ends meet. He testifies:

  "Just for fun, I used Psycho-Image Materialization to get money to burn. I've always wanted to be rich, you know? I pictured myself in an expensive car, always surrounded by beautiful girls— blondes, brunettes and redheads—in spite of the fact that I was working for peanuts! I saw myself skydiving, swimming, water skiing, skin diving— wonderful and marvelous fun things. One day during my Psycho-Image exercises, something changed. I can't really explain that. Suddenly I saw myself skin diving, but I 'saw' a treasure chest on the ocean floor. For no reason I can ever explain to a rationalist, I followed the impulse to go to that spot and dive. I did and I found the chest, just like in my Psycho-Image. It was a little smaller than I remembered, but it contained a sack of rotting leather. In it I discovered thirty gold coins, which turned out to be 63 ounces of pure gold. I cashed them in when gold was selling for $754 an ounce. Figure it out—I got over $47,000! Am I having fun? You bet I am!"

- Jim P., of Wheeling, West Virginia, was a worried man when economic troubles attacked the company he

worked for. Rumor had it that giant lay-offs were
about to begin and Jim felt like his "head was going to
roll." Yet he persisted in his Psycho-Image Materialization exercises, enjoying everyday benefits from it.
Sure enough, men started getting laid off, one after
the other.

Jim complained: "I've given my all to this company. I worked overtime. I even contributed ideas to
the company's suggestion box; that's how interested
I've been! Now they're going to fire me? Is this the
thanks a guy gets for being true?"

As in most cases of worry, Jim's negative emotions were unnecessary and, in reality, uncalled for.
Once Psycho-Image Materialization started working
for him, it never stopped. He learned this a few weeks
later (a few weeks of dread!) when not only was he *not*
laid off, but he was *promoted*! All those lay-offs
created new jobs. Duties had to be doubled up and
someone had to do the work. Jim was chosen as one of
the employees to stay on—promoted and given a fat
raise! Jim's reaction? "I haven't laughed in years," he
said. "Now I giggle like a happy kid!"

- Don R., of El Paso, Texas, a 14-year-old boy, started
  using Psycho-Image Materialization because his
  mother was using it. He joyfully reported that he got a
  longed-for bicycle by Psycho-Imaging himself on one.

- Roberta L., of Lincoln, Nebraska, uses Psycho-Image
  Materialization to obtain all the fun things she's always
  wanted but thought she couldn't have because of financial conditions. She wrote: "For a housewife with four
  children and a supposedly humdrum life, I'm having
  barrels of fun now. Thank you for Psycho-Image Materialization."

Let New Miracle Dynamics Work for You and Enjoy a Totally New And Exciting Life

Practice Psycho-Image Materialization as described in
this chapter and start now to fill your days and nights with

more fun and pleasure. The more you practice, the easier the practice becomes, and you will begin using Psycho-Image Materialization like a second nature, each and every day, in every situation. You'll see: more smiles will appear on your face, your eyes will take on a twinkle, and people around you will notice that you are getting fun out of life.

This chapter is geared to help you enjoy yourself. But it has another motive: It is preparing your subconscious to help you get *anything* you want! If you have read this far and have practiced the programs and techniques outlined in the foregoing chapters, you are ready to put Psycho-Image Materialization to the ultimate test—the acquisition of anything and everything you want, need, and desire.

Read on. Absorb. Practice. And be thankful prior to receipt. Then nothing need ever again be denied you. You will have all you want at your very fingertips, and you will receive what you want without physical effort—automatically, almost magically!

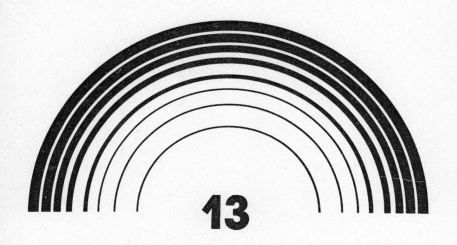

Obtain Everything You Want, Need, and Desire Through New Miracle Dynamics

Picture It: You are able to breathe under water. You are standing on the ocean floor, immersed in the water thousands of feet below the surface. You are enfolded, surrounded by water. All the nourishing minerals and vitamins in the sea permeate your body and infuse you with energy. You lack for nothing.

This Psycho-Image is an accurate portrayal of the truth of your being. You live in a cosmic sea of indefatigable mind power. You are surrounded and nourished by great mystical forces that the average person little understands and knows not how to use.

The miracle-working power of Psycho-Image Materialization, which issues from Universal Mind, is filtered through your own subconscious through the methods provided for you throughout this book.

The many Affirmations and Mind Activators are "programs" designed to give you the maximum benefit of Mind Power. By consciously using these techniques, you avail yourself of wonder-working abilities and "gifts from God." Claim them!

Your subconscious is the connecting link between your conscious mind and Universal Mind—and Psycho-Image Materialization is your tool for activating Mind in your personal life.

You will achieve direct contact with Mind each time you recite or mentalize an Affirmation and follow it with the practice of a Mind Activator. In time, your good will be automatic. Your whole life will change for the better. You will be pleased and amazed and delighted.

How to Take Full Advantage of the Secret of Psycho-Image Materialization for Your Own Benefit and Good

1. Psycho-Imagery is your key to trigger the generous giving of Universal Mind, causing it to release into your personal life all its goodness and riches.

Picture It: You receive wisdom and knowledge from a Higher Power, as blind men received sight from Christ.

2. You are thankful prior to receipt and you are willing to demonstrate your gratitude.

   For instance: If you receive a free automobile, you will use it ten percent of the time to transport people who have no car. If you receive a huge sum of money, you will give ten percent to charity or to a needy family. If you receive love and friendship, you will see to it that others receive your love and friendship.

   Here's the secret: What goes around, comes around!

3. God works through people! He wants all men and women to have abundant life. He conveys His goodness through those He blesses. *Picture It:* You are successful, wealthy, healthy, and knowledgeable, and now—out of gratitude—you will share your success, wealth, health, and knowledge with those less fortunate than you.

4. *Picture It:* You are a radiant, magnetic, charming, popular person. Your kindness, understanding, insight, and advice are widely sought. In gestures of great humility and thankfulness, you willingly and eagerly share all you have with others. You even share your Psycho-Image Materialization abilities. When you see someone suffering financial difficulties, love problems, or whatever trouble that individual may have, you Psycho-Image that person as healthy, wealthy, whole, and perfect.

Now you are ready to use Psycho-Image Materialization to obtain anything and everything you need.

Amazing New Miracle Dynamics Works Wonders Instantaneously

The moment you start practicing the following Psycho-Image Materialization Affirmation, you are already contacting and motivating Higher Powers to aid you.

In these final pages of the most powerful book you'll ever own, you are going to start accruing all the things you ever wanted in life.

Here is the secret that the quietly wealthy will not expose to the public—the magic use of Mind that turns thought into matter, desires into reality. You are provided with the Psycho-Image law that brings to you anything you can *picture* and infuse in your powerful subconscious. This law makes it possible for you to reap a harvest of riches, love, popularity, peace, and power—quickly and easily.

First, the subconscious-stirring Affirmation.

Psycho-Image Materialization Affirmation #13

Universal Mind already knows my needs, wants, hopes, and desires. Universal Mind is already the Source of everything I wish to have. As I turn my life and my will over to the care of Higher Powers, my every wish is granted.

No person, place, or thing can keep me from the fulfillment of my dreams. All good flows freely as honey because I am a willing servant of God. I share my great abundance with all people. I wish all good for others, as well as myself. I believe, trust, and know that Universal Mind will work through people to help me, support me, lift me, and enrich me.

Universal Mind is the sole Source of my good, not outside influences or conditions. As I open through Psycho-Image Materialization exercises, the Power of Mind manifests and demonstrates my good before my very eyes. I willingly turn my attention from people, places, and things and accept that they are channels of the Source, not the Source Itself.

I am richly supplied, even far beyond my hopes and dreams. I am prosperous and successful in everything I undertake to do. Whatever

I touch turns to gold as if by magic. Nothing but good comes to me and I give nothing but good to others. I move forward now in Psycho-Image Materialization to claim all that I want, need, desire, and hope for.

I am eternally grateful for this contact with an all-loving, all-giving Higher Power. I am now thankful for the many good things about to manifest abundantly in my life.

How to Encourage the Powerful Creative Force of the Universe to Produce Your Good

The above Affirmation will prepare your subconscious mind to receive your potent Psycho-Images. It is vital that you dispel all negativity in your mind, heart, body, and atmosphere. The way to do this is itself Psycho-Image Materialization.

Picture It: You are strolling through a beautiful park on a balmy summer day. Flowers are radiantly beautiful everywhere you look, the grass is gorgeously green, and a calming, gentle breeze wafts through the healthy leaves of many trees.

Picture It: You are sitting on a huge boulder, overlooking the sea. Watch the seagulls swoop and glide over the rippling waves. See the reflection of the setting sun in the water. Feel at-one with the halcyon scene.

Picture It: You are in thick, rich woods, sitting beside an ambling brook. Hear the streaming water babble and gurgle as it cascades over the rocks. Smell the aroma of lovely flowers. Hear bees buzzing. Listen to the breeze moving trees. Breathe deeply of the fresh, invigorating air.

In this state of mind, at peace, in tranquility, you are ready to charge your subconscious with energy.

new Miracle Dynamics Mind Activator #13

1. You will now "draw down" the potent psychic energy that is needed in your subconscious. You will attract it from the vital force in which you are immersed. To become conscious of this invisible but powerful force is to be in a position to channel it.

2. Sit or lie down comfortably. Begin a slow inhaling and exhaling process. With each exhalation, say:
   I breathe out lack and limitation.
   With each inhalation, say:
   I breathe in plenty and boundless good.
   Do this ten times.

3. Extend your arms and hold your right hand, palm downward, directly over your left hand, palm upward, about six inches apart. Very slowly, close the gap until your hands almost touch. Don't let them touch. Draw them away from one another again to a distance of about six inches. Now with each inhalation, draw them apart, and with each exhalation bring them close. Do this until you can actually feel energy building up like a ball between your hands. This is a concentrated field of super energy that you will actually use.

4. Just as if you had a ball between your hands, lift the energy to the top of your head and set it there. Balance the ball of energy on the top of your head.

5. *Picture It:* The ball of energy is melting!

> The solid object is liquifying, but the liquid is not dripping over you; it is seeping *into* your brain, activating it, motivating it, energizing it.
>
> 6. When your mind is saturated with cosmic energy, plant your wish, need, or desire into it. Do this by Psycho-Imaging exactly what you want. Immediately express your gratitude for the fulfillment of your desire. *Picture It:* You are kneeling before God and smiling in thankfulness. This Psycho-Image will work.
>
> 7. Now say these words:
>   *It is done. Amen. The seed I have planted in divine soil will manifest as good in my life. Thank You!*

"Ask and you shall receive" is not a quaint phrase but an inexorable cosmic law and Psycho-Image Materialization puts it into action for you.

It does not matter what it is you want. Universal Mind does not pick and choose what It will give you. *You* determine what you want, and Universal Mind automatically provides it! When you know *how* to ask for something, you get it—easily and quickly. "Asking" means communicating with higher than human Power, and such questions must always be put in the form of Psycho-Images. A picture is worth more than ten thousand words—it is the difference between wishing and having.

As you develop expertise in seeding your subconscious with Psycho-Images, you will start reaping a harvest of untold riches and happiness—anything you want! There is nothing—absolutely nothing—in my life that was not first seeded in my subconscious with Psycho-Images. And thousands of others are using this amazing path to success and happiness.

Terry M. Wanted a Beautiful Girl and Employed Psycho-Imagery to Get What He Wanted

Terry M., of Wichita, Kansas, was a lonely bachelor with big ideas about gorgeous females. Like many men, he wanted companionship, fun, love, and fulfillment. Unlike other men, he got what he wanted! His buddies were astounded when he showed up at a party with a voluptuous, ripe peach of a girl, a veritable model. How did he attract such a vivacious woman?

His Psycho-Image technique was simple, and you can use it, too—if not to attract a girl, then to attract anything you want.

Every evening after work, Terry cut out paper dolls! Now why would a grown man do a thing like that? Because he learned the secret of how Psycho-Images activate potent subconscious powers. Each night he collected photos of beautiful, sexy females from magazines. Sometimes he clipped whole covers from such magazines as *Cosmopolitan* and glued all of them in a photograph album.

This is the essence of the Psycho-Image method of attracting what you want. No movement is idle. You see, as Terry cut out the pictures, set them in order, pasted them into his album, accumulated hundreds of them, he was *at the same time* seeding his subconscious, sending out attractive vibrations and setting up the right psychic atmosphere for realization of his dream. That's how it works.

You can do exactly the same thing. If you need a mate, man or woman, use the same technique, saving dozens of pictures of the kind of person you would like to be associated with.

Maybe you want a new home. Use magazines like *House and Garden*. Accumulate scores of lovely photos of rich and luxurious homes. As you immerse yourself in this private collection, your subconscious will become attuned to your desire—and it will fulfill it in ways you never dreamed of!

Do you want a new car? Follow the same procedure, only this time collect pictures of fabulous automobiles!

Whatever you desire, this method works, just as it worked for Terry, a most happy man!

How Audrey B. Used Psycho-Image Materialization to Gain Fabulous Wealth

Audrey B., of Tucson, Arizona, had a problem shared by millions of other people: she was flat broke and desperate for enough money to live on. When she learned about Psycho-Image Materialization, she used the backs of her eyelids for a "movie screen" and "saw" movies of her hopes and dreams. Again and again, she replayed her mental film of herself gaining vast amounts of money in all sorts of ways. It doesn't matter how you picture yourself receiving things; the picturing is the seeding of your subconscious and it will act.

An outdoors girl, Audrey went horseback riding one lovely afternoon, out into the desert area to be alone with her Psycho-Images. As she rode along, her horse stumbled and Audrey was thrown. Screaming in fright, she tumbled down a bank and fell into the mouth of a cave. Sand filtered away and the entrance was revealed. Audrey gathered her wits and looked around in startled amazement. She found herself sitting among rare jewels, hunks of jade, gold pieces, ivory icons, and hundreds of other precious objects. She had "stumbled" into an ancient tomb and unearthed thousands of dollars worth of artifacts. She was paid the healthy sum of $450,000 for her discovery! She said confidently:

> "I just know I was *led* to that spot. My Higher Power guided me there as surely as It guides the stars in their courses. I was ready, that's all. I'd been using Psycho-Image Materialization for six months when it happened. No wonder my worries are over. This system works!"

Even that huge sum of money is not the end of Audrey's windfall. An archaeology magazine pays her regularly for articles on her find. A nature magazine commissioned her to do a story on the desert treasure. Even a horse-lovers periodical wants her articles. Money hasn't stopped coming to Audrey since she started Psycho-Imaging herself as wealthy.

Apply New Miracle Dynamics, and You Will Have Your Heart's Desire

Now that you have reached the end of our remarkable, wonder-working system, start over! Yes, begin at the beginning of this book and start reading once more. Implant the secrets of this book in your subconscious mind, and I guarantee that you will be one happy, fulfilled, grateful human being. So be it!

A Final Word About New Miracle Dynamics

Contact Higher Power through New Miracle Dynamics and reap your harvest of success and happiness. Claim your good! Know your worth! Know once and for all that your subconscious is a vast reservoir of infinite riches at your fingertips, ready to do your bidding.

Of course, concentration is required; but not labor. Yes, you need to practice Psycho-Image Materialization; but you don't have to sweat. Repetition is indeed a must; but you can do the easy steps right in the comfort of your home, even on coffee breaks at work. The rewards are so great for so little effort.

Feel immersed in a world-embracing Power that wants nothing but good for you. Declare your right to love, wealth, power, health, success, joy, friendship—for all these and more are yours for the asking through Psycho-Imagery. If you want any or all of these things . . .

Picture It!